1st Healthcare® Compliance **HIPAA Privacy and Security**

ISBN: 978-0-9991797-1-0

Published by First Healthcare Compliance, LLC.

To order additional copies or to learn more about First Healthcare Compliance, call us at 888.54.FIRST (888.543.4778) or visit our website at www.1sthcc.com.

Table of Contents

Introduction

For today's healthcare providers, the Health Insurance Portability and Accountability Act (HIPAA) is an unavoidable part of doing business. Compliance requires carefully planned and executed policies and procedures, as well as a significant investment of time, resources and expertise.

Healthcare providers have voiced concerns that HIPAA-related activities put an unreasonable strain on their operations and interfere with their core mission of providing patient care. However, as companies struggle to establish reasonable ways to share and manage an ever-growing volume of sensitive patient data, they recognize that, although imperfect, HIPAA provides them with the needed framework for addressing this critical issue, which, at the end of the day, is of a piece with providing quality care to patients.

It is difficult to overstate the devastating consequences that can result when a patient's privacy has been violated. Patients who have been the victims of privacy violations have reported losing their jobs; becoming estranged from friends, family, or their community; having their reputations damaged; even becoming the targets of blackmail. Privacy violations can also result in identity theft, which can require arduous and costly measures to resolve.

Confidentiality is also essential for providing effective care to patients. Patients who do not trust their healthcare provider to keep their personal information confidential will be hesitant to reveal information about themselves or family members for fear that it could leak out. This lack of trust interferes with medical care, because a patient might opt to hold back critical details that the caregiver needs to effectively treat the patient.

When discussing HIPAA with healthcare providers, we typically start by asking the providers to think of themselves as patients. We ask them to consider how much they value their own privacy and how much havoc a breach of confidential information could cause in their own personal lives.

We then turn to how a privacy or security breach can affect their business operations. Lax compliance and cutting corners can be costly and potentially crippling for companies, not only because of steep fines and penalties, but also because of enduring damage to the company's reputation.

The best strategy for addressing these real concerns for the patient and for the provider is to understand the rules and requirements, and put together a thoughtful plan that can be successfully implemented to stay in compliance and keep patient data safe.

Our aim with this book is to make that task a little easier. For the past six years, First Healthcare Compliance has been providing healthcare organizations with the compliance management solution they need to manage HIPAA and other healthcare compliance requirements. During that time, our team of experts has also provided clients with valuable compliance resources, such as toll-free support, weekly blogs and newsletters, a webinar and podcast series, and most recently, an online healthcare compliance course and companion handbook called ***First Healthcare Compliance The Fundamentals***.

Since then, we've heard from healthcare professionals, members of the legal community, and teachers looking for a hands-on resource that focusses on HIPAA. Those requests drove us to develop this newest resource, ***First Healthcare Compliance HIPAA Privacy and Security***.

The book is designed to provide an easy-to-understand overview of HIPAA and how it impacts healthcare organizations and their employees. We've taken special care to alert readers to particular elements of HIPAA that should be kept top of mind, and to provide context with specific examples of HIPAA-related situations.

The book explores how HIPAA Rules impact healthcare providers, provides the key components of a HIPAA compliance plan, and explains the consequences of HIPAA noncompliance. It begins with a brief history of HIPAA before tackling the HIPAA Privacy Rule, the HIPAA Security Rule, The Health Information Technology for Economic and Clinical Health (HITECH) Act, and Enforcement. The book's appendices include sample forms as well as suggestions for further reading.

Throughout the book, readers will find specific examples, resources, and suggested activities to help process and understand the information.

We welcome your questions and the opportunity to assist you with additional resource materials and compliance services. Please don't hesitate to contact us with thoughts or questions.

The First Healthcare Compliance Team
888.54.FIRST
www.1sthcc.com

Healthcare® Compliance First Healthcare Compliance HIPAA Privacy and Security *is designed to be an easy-to-understand, up-to-date reference to assist you with healthcare compliance concerns. However, this companion guide is not intended as legal advice, which will depend on facts, circumstances, and applicable law. The intricacies of this area of the law can result in serious penalties if a violation occurs. Readers should consider this book a starting point in this complex process and contact an attorney for legal advice, if needed.*

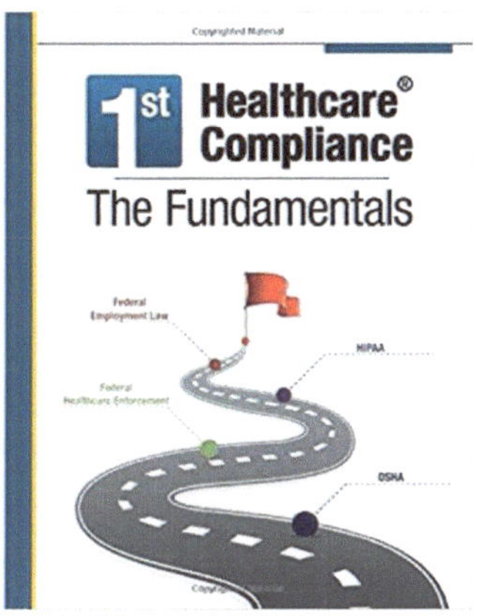

First Healthcare Compliance The Fundamentals is a comprehensive resource designed to help physicians, compliance professionals and other healthcare professionals in private practice, hospital networks and health systems, healthcare billing companies and skilled nursing facilities comply with federal rules and regulations and to better understand their compliance responsibilities at a time of heightened scrutiny and increased regulations. The book addresses the four major areas of healthcare compliance regulations: HIPAA, OSHA, federal waste and abuse laws, and federal employment laws. It can be used as a stand-alone resource or as a companion guide to the *First Healthcare Compliance The Fundamentals* online course.

About the Authors

Sheba Vine, JD, CP, CIPP/US

Sheba Vine is a lawyer and privacy professional that has written articles in the areas of privacy, human resource compliance, and healthcare laws. Sheba is certified by the International Association of Privacy Professionals (IAPP) as a Certified Information Privacy Professional (CIPP/US). Sheba worked in private practice, concentrating in litigation and employment laws. Prior to her legal career, Sheba held positions in the medical device industry with Hoffman La-Roche and Siemens. She received her Juris Doctorate from Widener University School of Law and her Bachelor of Science in Biomedical Engineering from Drexel University and is licensed to practice law in Delaware, New Jersey, Pennsylvania and before the U.S. Patent and Trademark Office.

Julie Sheppard BSN, JD, CHC
President and Founder, First Healthcare Compliance

Julie Sheppard is a nurse, an attorney, and certified in Healthcare Compliance by the Compliance Certification Board. Married to a physician, her understanding of healthcare compliance issues grew from education, experience, and personal interest. With the increase in compliance challenges facing healthcare providers, Julie was inspired to create a practical, comprehensive healthcare compliance solution, and founded First Healthcare Compliance in 2012. Julie's professional memberships include the Pennsylvania Bar Association, the American Health Lawyers Association, and the Healthcare Compliance Association.

About First Healthcare Compliance

1st Healthcare® Compliance

First Healthcare Compliance helps healthcare organizations of every size comply with an increasingly complex regulatory environment. Our software solution creates confidence among compliance professionals through education, resources, and support in the areas of HIPAA, OSHA, human resources compliance, and fraud waste and abuse laws. Serving clients across the United States, the company's evolving platform provides real-time insight for board reporting and across multiple locations. For more information please visit https://1sthcc.com/.

Chapter 1

A History of HIPAA

Overview

In this chapter, you will learn how the HIPAA Privacy, Security, and Enforcement Rules evolved. You will also learn how privacy and security are different but related, and you will learn how states address HIPAA laws. This chapter also provides you with a list of abbreviations and acronyms that will be used frequently in this book.

Chapter Outline

1.1 HIPAA's origins
1.2 The HITECH Act
1.3 The Omnibus Rule
1.4 Understanding privacy versus security
1.5 State laws and how they relate to HIPAA
1.6 A guide to HIPAA terms and abbreviations used in this book

Learning Objectives

After completing this chapter, you should be able to do the following:

- ✓ Explain the circumstances that led to the development of HIPAA, HITECH, and the Omnibus Rule.
- ✓ Understand how patient data privacy and security are related.
- ✓ Understand how state laws interpret HIPAA.
- ✓ Be familiar with the terms, acronyms, and government agencies discussed in this book.

1.1 HIPAA History

Although patient privacy has always been a concern for healthcare professionals, a legal vacuum existed for many years in the U.S. with regard to safeguarding confidential health data. A hodgepodge of federal and state laws left gaps that allowed for the distribution of personal health information without notice or authorization, often for reasons that had nothing to do with treatment or insurance.

Such gaps meant that patients were vulnerable to having their private health information used for purposes that they neither authorized nor sought, for example, by employers for personnel decisions, financial lenders, life insurance companies, and others.

Things came to a head in the early 1990s as healthcare companies began to anticipate the shift to digital records and the electronic transfer of information. Lawmakers recognized the need for a comprehensive legal framework that would modernize the flow of health information to keep it safe while making it available to authorized users such as doctors, nurses, hospitals, and insurance companies. They also took advantage of the occasion to address another pressing healthcare concern: the ability for people to hold onto their health insurance when they lost or changed jobs.

In 1996, Senators Ted Kennedy (D-Mass.) and Nancy Kassebaum (R-Kan.) introduced a bill into Congress to address issues of healthcare privacy, security, and portability. The bill, initially named after the sponsoring senators but later changed to The Health Insurance Portability and Accountability Act (HIPAA), was enacted by Congress on August 21, 1996 and signed soon after by President Bill Clinton.

HIPAA Titles

Title	Topics addressed
Title I	Healthcare access and portability
Title II	Includes the Administrative Simplification Rules, which establish policies and procedures regarding the privacy and security of individually identifiable health information (IIHI), and require the creation of standards for using and sharing healthcare information. Title II also addresses healthcare fraud and abuse and medical liability reform.
Title III	The use of pre-tax medical savings accounts
Title IV	addresses medical coverage for employees with pre-existing medical conditions
Title V	Company-owned life insurance policies

The Act consisted of five titles that addressed a range of healthcare issues, from access to portability to the use of pre-tax medical savings accounts. (Note: This book focuses on three of the five Administrative Simplification rules in Title II: The Privacy Rule, the Security Rule, and the Enforcement Rule. The book also addresses the changes to HIPAA made by the HITECH Act and Omnibus Rule.)

1.1.1 A HIPAA timeline

Although the Act was passed and signed in August 1996, it took much longer to finalize due to its complexity and later due to the 2000 elections and changes in the administration.

Following the initial passage of the Act, the US Department of Health and Human Services (HHS), the agency charged with creating standards for the use and disclosure of healthcare information and for enforcing HIPAA, submitted preliminary recommendations for federal health privacy legislation to Congress in 1997. Congress was unable to enact privacy legislation and as a result, HHS was required to issue regulations.

The regulations were then finalized in parts. The first was the Transaction and Code Sets final rule creating health data exchange standards, which was published in August 2000 and became effective in 2002. HHS published a Final Privacy Rule in December 2000, which was modified in August 2002 and became effective in 2003. The Privacy Rule protected personal health information (PHI) and mandated a patient signature prior to the release of information, except for treatment, payment, and healthcare operations (TPO). The HIPAA Security Rule was published in 2003 and became effective in 2005. The Security Rule established a national set of security standards for personal health information (PHI) in electronic format.

In addition to the detailed guidelines and instructions regarding how PHI should be disclosed, stored, and shared, HIPAA established the consequences of noncompliance. Despite the threat of significant monetary penalties, healthcare providers were initially slow to comply with the HIPAA Privacy and Security Rules, prompting the introduction of the Enforcement Rule in 2006, followed by the Breach Notification Rule.

The Enforcement Rule clarified and elaborated on the power of HHS to investigate regulated healthcare entities accused of failing to comply with the Privacy Rule, provided the bases for liability, and also clarified how to determine the amount of the penalties for failing to follow Security Rule safeguards that resulted in breaches of electronic protected health information (ePHI). In addition, it set out grounds for waiver, conduct of the hearing, and the appeal process.

In 2009, Congress signed the HITECH Act (see Section 1.2) to reinforce the Security Rule, and in 2013, HHS issued the Omnibus Final Rule (see Section 1.3) to implement HITECH in order to improve data security, further restrict access to ePHI, and compel the business associates (BAs) of entities covered by HIPAA to also comply with certain requirements, among other things.

HHS' Office for Civil Rights (OCR) was designated as the agency responsible for enforcing the Privacy, Security, and Breach Notification Rules. A series of audits conducted by OCR in 2011 and 2012 found serious HIPAA compliance issues throughout the healthcare industry. OCR provided entities that were not in compliance with action plans to help them get compliant, and warned entities that subsequent audits would be less forgiving.

The Evolution of HIPAA

August 1996	Congress passes HIPAA; the process to modernize the flow of health information begins
August 1998	The Security Rule is proposed
November 1999	The Privacy Rule is proposed
December 2000	HHS issues the Privacy Rule
2001-2002	A new administration comes in and HIPAA is halted; the comment period is opened again the next year with the agreement to add exceptions to Privacy Rule for treatment, payment and healthcare operations
February 2003	HHS issues the Security Rule
April 2003	The Privacy Rule goes into effect; companies must begin compliance (small companies have until April 2004)
October 2003	The Transactions and Code Sets Rule goes into effect
April 2005	The Security Rule goes into effect (small companies have until April 2006); the Enforcement Rule is proposed
March 2006	The Enforcement Rule goes into effect
February 2009	HITECH signed into law, Breach Notification Rule introduced
August 2009	Breach Notifications Interim Regulations are issued
February 2010	HITECH enforcement begins
March 2012	The Omnibus Final Rule is finalized
January 2013	The Omnibus Final Rule is issued, and takes effect two months later

Beginning in 2011, OCR began an audit program to assess the HIPAA compliance efforts of covered entities (CEs). In 2016, OCR launched phase 2 of the audit program, which reviewed HIPAA policies and procedures used by CEs and their BAs. In its preliminary findings for CEs released in September 2017, the OCR found that few entities had fully met compliance goals. None of the audited entities had conducted meaningful security risk analysis. Access request and Notice of Privacy Practices (NPP) management were other problem areas.

In addition to negative audit findings, there have been a number of costly HIPAA settlements, fines and penalties in the last five years. For example, two healthcare companies paid combined fines of nearly $8 million in 2018. That was in addition to the costs of issuing breach notifications, providing credit monitoring services and other damage mitigation to the organizations' operations and their reputations.

Such incidents, and the certainty of new rounds of OCR audits, are compelling healthcare providers and their BAs at large and small organizations to be more aggressive with compliance efforts, including incorporating training and technology.

1.2 The HITECH Act

The Security Rule was reinforced with the passage of The Health Information Technology for Economic and Clinical Health (HITECH) Act, enacted as part of the American Recovery and Reinvestment Act of 2009. Introduced during the Obama administration as part of an economic stimulus package, the HITECH Act was primarily created to promote and expand the adoption of health information technology among healthcare companies in an effort to control healthcare costs by incentivizing them to share information. The Act also served to strengthen HIPAA Privacy and Security Rules.

1.2.1 Breach notification

The HITECH Act mandated breach notification rules by requiring notification to patients, the government, and the media based on the number of individuals impacted by a breach of unsecured PHI.

Under the HITECH Act, CEs must provide notice to all patients whose information has been breached. The notice must include what happened and the steps that the CE is taking to resolve the breach. (See Chapter 6 for more on HIPAA breach notification.)

1.2.2 Electronic health record access

The HITECH Act gave patients the right to obtain their electronic personal health information (ePHI) in an electronic format from any provider that uses an electronic health record (EHR) system, or to authorize a third party to receive their ePHI. The Act allowed healthcare providers to charge patients for providing the ePHI, but the charges could only equal the labor costs needed to complete the request.

1.2.3 Business associates

The HITECH Act made significant changes to HIPAA liability for BAs, the entities that partner with or provide services to healthcare companies covered by HIPAA.

Learn more about BAs

Business Associates: Section 2.2.2
BA Agreements: Section 5.7.1
Handling a BA breach: Section 8.8

Until 2009, BAs were not held directly liable for HIPAA violations. The HITECH Act changed that, requiring BAs to comply with the Security Rule, including implementing administrative, physical and technical safeguards. BAs also have to comply with portions of the Privacy Rule. In addition, BAs became subject to audits and penalties for HIPAA violations.

Subcontractors hired by BAs carry the same responsibilities as the BAs themselves for any activities related to the creation, maintenance, and/or transmission of ePHI.

1.2.4 Fundraising/marketing

The HITECH Act established provisions for ePHI accounting of disclosures for fundraising and marketing activities. For example, the HITECH Act required that fundraising communications efforts comply with HIPAA Privacy requirements, and it required healthcare entities covered by HIPAA to obtain proper authorization for the use or disclosure of PHI used for marketing purposes, or for the sale of PHI.

HIPAA violations that occurred as a result of noncompliance with the HITECH Act carried significant financial penalties, which increased even more with the Final Omnibus Rule.

1.3 The Omnibus Final Rule

In 2013, HHS published the HIPAA Omnibus Rule, a set of final regulations that established compliance with HITECH Act regulations and made final modifications to the HIPAA Privacy, Security, Enforcement, and Breach Notification Rules.

The Omnibus Rule contained the most significant modifications to the HIPAA Privacy and Security Rules since their inception, further strengthening patient privacy protections and giving patients additional rights regarding their PHI.

Notable Omnibus regulations that implemented the HITECH Act mandates and HIPAA regulations included the following:

- BAs were made directly liable for compliance with certain HIPAA Privacy and Security Rules requirements.

- Penalties for HIPAA violations increased to up to $1.5 million per violation, and tiered civil monetary penalties were introduced.
- Breach notification protocols were finalized.
- Individuals' rights were expanded to allow them to receive electronic copies of their health information.
- The limitations on the use and disclosure of PHI for marketing and fundraising purposes were strengthened, and the sale of PHI was prohibited without individual authorization.
- Modifications to, and redistribution of, a CE's NPP were required.
- The individual authorization requirement and others were modified to facilitate research and disclosure of child immunization proof to schools, and to enable access to the health information of deceased individuals by family members or other authorized parties.
- Enhancements to the Enforcement Rule were adopted, including provisions addressing enforcement of noncompliance with the HIPAA Rules due to willful neglect.
- The Rule authorized attorneys to bring civil actions to enforce HIPAA.

1.4 Privacy and Security

HIPAA addresses both the privacy and the security of PHI. Under HIPAA, privacy focuses on the patient. It refers to a patient's right to limit individual health information from being used, disclosed or shared without the patient's consent. Although there are exceptions that allow CEs to disclose PHI, patients can expect that their healthcare providers will take the measures necessary to ensure their PHI is kept private and confidential.

The HIPAA Privacy Rule outlines the rights of the individual with regard to PHI and establishes standards for the electronic exchange, privacy, and security of health information. The Rule requires CEs to create and implement a comprehensive compliance plan to keep all types of PHI—paper, oral and electronic—safe and confidential.

Security refers to the ways that CEs *achieve* PHI privacy, that is, the tools, policies and procedures they use to keep PHI safe from unauthorized disclosure, access, loss or destruction.

The HIPAA Security Rule complements the Privacy Rule by providing guidelines on how CEs can safely share and store ePHI, the subset of PHI in electronic form. The Rule provides for more comprehensive security requirements than the Privacy Rule with regard to ePHI.

1.5 HIPAA and State Law

Many states already had privacy laws on the books before HIPAA came about. Some states went on to pass new laws once HIPAA took effect to further strengthen privacy protections and increase punishments. As a result, healthcare providers are sometimes unsure about their compliance obligations with regard to state and federal regulations.

According to HHS, the Privacy Rule was designed to address this concern and to minimize conflicts between state and federal requirements. Generally, federal law supersedes state law when dealing with the privacy and security of confidential health information, unless state law is more stringent when dealing with PHI. In such cases, CEs should comply with the state laws that provide greater protections for PHI and greater privacy rights for individuals.

Always check state laws

Healthcare providers should familiarize themselves with the laws of their home state and conduct further research to determine whether there are any areas of conflict between their state laws and HIPAA. Potential points of concern include time lengths/deadlines; monetary fines; allowable uses and disclosures of PHI; and patients' rights..

The Privacy Rule lists three exceptions where CEs can use or disclose PHI in cases where federal and state law do not align:

- The state law relates to the privacy of individual identifiable health information (IIHI) and provides greater privacy protections or privacy rights with respect to the information.
- The state law provides for the reporting of disease or injury, child abuse, birth, or death, or for public health surveillance, investigation, or intervention.
- The state law requires certain health plan reporting, such as for management or financial audits. In these circumstances, a CE is not required to comply with a "contrary" provision of the Privacy Rule.

Note that only state laws that are "contrary" to federal requirements are eligible for an exemption determination. Contrary means that it would be impossible for a CE to comply with both the state and federal requirements, or that the state law is an obstacle to accomplishing the full purposes and objectives of HIPAA. For example, Texas House Bill 300 provides stricter requirements for CEs and an expanded definition of "covered entity" that encompasses anyone who creates, receives, maintains and transmits PHI.

1.6 HIPAA Terms and Acronyms

Acronyms, agencies and abbreviations are frequently used when discussing HIPAA. Below are some of the most commonly-used terms and abbreviations. Some terms are self-explanatory; others will be addressed in subsequent chapters.

Term	Description
Business Associate (BA)	A person or entity that performs certain functions or activities that involve the use or disclosure of PHI on behalf of, or provides services to, a CE
Business Associate Agreement (BAA)	A covered entity's contract or other written arrangement with its business associate
Covered Entity (CE)	Health plans, healthcare clearinghouses, and healthcare providers that electronically transmit health information
Department of Justice (DOJ)	Works in conjunction with the OCR on possible HIPAA criminal violations
Department of Health and Human Services (HHS)	Administers HIPAA at the national level
Designated Record Set	A group of records maintained by or for a covered entity
Electronic Data Interchange (EDI)	The electronic transfer of medical, billing, and other HIPAA-covered information among CEs and BAs.
Electronic Health Record (EHR)	Electronic versions of patients' paper records kept by healthcare providers, such as medical history and physicians' notes; also known as Electronic Medical Records (EMR)
Electronic Protected Health Information (ePHI)	PHI that is stored and shared in electronic format
Health Insurance Portability Act of 1996 (HIPAA)	Provides data privacy and security provisions for safeguarding medical information
Health Information Technology for Economic and Clinical Health Act (HITECH)	Created to stimulate the adoption of electronic health records (EHR) and the supporting technology in the United States
Hybrid Entity	An entity that performs some functions that are covered by HIPAA and other functions that are not.
Individually Identifiable Health Information (IIHI)	Health information that can be linked to a specific person, or could be used to identify a person; PHI is a subset of IIHI
Non-covered entities (Non-CEs)	An entity that does not meet the definition of a covered entity or business associate, and does not have to comply with HIPAA
Notice of Privacy Practices (NPP)	Provides a clear, user-friendly explanation of individuals' rights with respect to their personal health information and the privacy practices of CEs.
Office of Civil Rights (OCR)	An HHS agency responsible for enforcing the Privacy and Security Rules
Omnibus Final Rule	A set of final regulations modifying the HIPAA Privacy, Security, and Enforcement Rules to implement various provisions of the HITECH Act
Protected Health Information (PHI)	A subset of individually identifiable health information created or maintained by CEs and their BAs
Treatment, Payment, and Healthcare Operations (TPO)	The HIPAA Privacy Rule permits CEs to use and disclose PHI, with certain limits and protections, for these routine, core healthcare activities

Chapter 2

The HIPAA Privacy Rule

Overview

In this chapter, you will learn how the HIPAA Privacy Rule is defined and the business entity types that are covered by the Rule. You will also learn what is considered protected health information (PHI), how information can be "de-identified," and the permitted uses and disclosures of PHI. Finally, you will learn about PHI practices required by HIPAA.

Chapter Outline

2.1 Patient privacy
2.2 Entities addressed by HIPAA
2.3 Personal representatives
2.3 Protected health information
2.4 Permitted uses and disclosures of protected health information
2.5 Minimum necessary information requirement
2.6 Protected health information practices

Learning Objectives

After completing this chapter, you should be able to do the following:

- ✓ Explain the HIPAA Privacy Rule.
- ✓ List and describe the entities that are required to comply with HIPAA.
- ✓ Understand what is meant by PHI, as well as de-identified PHI and permitted uses and disclosures.
- ✓ Be familiar with the PHI practices required by HIPAA.

2.1 Patient Privacy

Physicians have long recognized the critical importance of protecting a patient's privacy. In addition to moral and ethical considerations, patient confidentiality is essential to achieving positive health outcomes. If patients are concerned that their medical details could become public knowledge, they might be reluctant to share health information, fearing that it might damage their reputation, put their job at risk or put them in danger. Patients and caregivers need a relationship built on trust and confidentiality if the care is to be effective.

As discussed in Chapter 1, the HIPAA Privacy Rule was designed to address this critical patient care issue—especially in light of the increased use of electronic storage and transfer of records. The Rule, the first comprehensive federal protection of the privacy of health information, created national standards to protect individuals' medical records and other personal health information (PHI).

Confidentiality between a caregiver and patient is a critical component of quality care.

The Privacy Rule requires certain healthcare providers to implement safeguards that protect the privacy of PHI, and regulates the ways that the providers can use and disclose PHI without a patient's authorization. The Rule also provides patients with rights over their health information, such as the right to examine their health records, to obtain a copy of them, and to request corrections.

The Privacy Rule was designed to do the following:

- It gives patients more control over their health information.
- It sets boundaries on the use and release of health records.
- It establishes safeguards that healthcare providers and others must implement to protect the privacy of health information.
- It holds violators accountable, with civil and criminal penalties that can be imposed for violating patients' privacy rights.
- It seeks to strike a balance when there is a public need for disclosure of some forms of data—for example, to protect public health.

The Privacy Rule also gives patients the ability to make informed choices when seeking care, and reimbursement for care, based on how their PHI may be used:

- It enables patients to find out how their PHI may be used, and to ask about certain PHI disclosures that have been made.

- It limits the release of information to the minimum necessary needed to achieve the intended purpose.
- It gives patients the right to examine and obtain a copy of their own health records and to request corrections.
- It empowers individuals to control certain uses and disclosures of their PHI.

2.2 Entities Addressed by HIPAA

The Privacy Rule establishes which entity types must comply with the HIPAA regulations, and it provides compliance guidelines.

The Rule distinguishes between HIPAA-covered and non-HIPAA covered entities (CEs). CEs include healthcare providers that perform standard electronic transactions, health plans, and healthcare clearinghouses. Third parties, known as business associates (BAs), that have access to patient information must also comply with HIPAA.

2.2.1 Covered entities

These are the entities that are required to comply with HIPAA rules:

- **Health plan:** With certain exceptions, a health plan is an individual or group plan that pays for medical care. The law specifically includes many types of organizations and government programs as health plans, such as insurance companies (individual or group), Medicare, Medicaid, Children's Health Insurance Program (CHIP), Civilian Health and Medical Program of the Uniformed Services (CHAMPUS), and prescription drug plans.
- **Healthcare clearinghouse:** A clearinghouse is a public or private entity—including a billing service, repricing company, community health management information system or community health information system and "value-added" networks and switches—that acts as a go-between for CEs (for example a healthcare provider and insurance company) to provide the following services:
    - Process or facilitate the processing of health information received from another entity in a nonstandard format or containing nonstandard data content into standard data elements or a standard transaction.
    - Receive a standard transaction from another entity to process or facilitate the processing of health information into nonstandard format or nonstandard data content for the receiving entity.

  For example: A healthcare claims clearinghouse would review an insurance claim for errors before submitting it to the payer, and then notify the healthcare provider that the claim has been accepted or denied.

- **Healthcare provider:** These are individuals, organizations or entities that provide, bill, or are paid for medical or health services as part of their business. Examples include doctors, nurses, dentists, psychologists, nursing homes, hospitals, and pharmacies. Healthcare refers to care, services, or supplies related to the health of an individual, including preventive, diagnostic, therapeutic, rehabilitative, maintenance, or palliative care, and counseling, service, assessment, or procedures with respect to the physical or mental condition, or functional status, of an individual; and the sale or dispensing of a drug, device, equipment, or other item requiring a prescription.
- **Affiliated covered entity:** Affiliated CEs are legally separate entities that are affiliated with a CE under common ownership. An example is an integrated delivery network that includes hospitals, medical groups, and long-term care facilities.
- **Organized healthcare arrangement:** There are certain operational arrangements among entities that require the participants to share PHI. An example would be doctors who are affiliated with a university faculty and treat patients in a hospital or health system. For the purposes of HIPAA, a key factor of determining whether an organized healthcare arrangement is a CE is if the patient is aware of the arrangement.

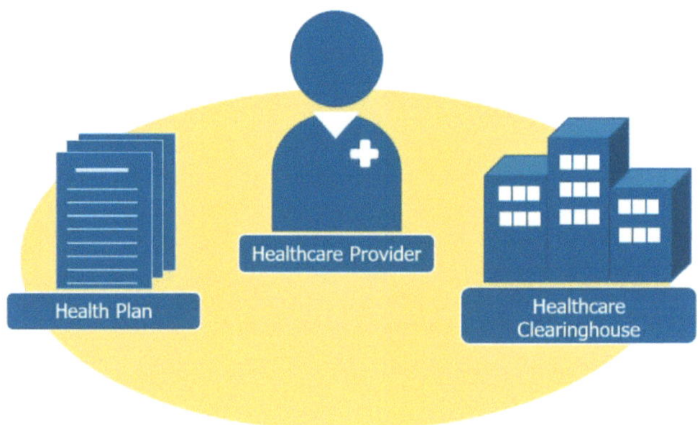

CEs have the ultimate responsibility to protect and secure. They are responsible for providing records and compliance reports and for cooperating with complaint investigations and compliance reviews by HHS, including permitting access to facilities, records, accounts, and PHI, if necessary, to determine whether the CE is in compliance with HIPAA regulations. CEs are also responsible for managing the relationship with BAs.

2.2.2 Business associates

A CE's BAs must also comply with HIPAA requirements. A BA is a person or an entity that is not part of the CE's workforce but performs activities on behalf of the CE that involve the use or disclosure of PHI.

The types of functions or activities for which a person or entity may be considered a BA include payment or healthcare operations activities, as well as many other functions or activities regulated by the Administrative Simplification Rules, such as legal, actuarial, accounting, consulting, data aggregation, management, administrative, accreditation, and financial services. Such activities include:

- Claims processing or administration
- Data analysis, processing, or administration
- Utilization review
- Quality assurance
- Billing
- Benefits management
- Practice management
- Repricing

Examples of BAs include:

- A third-party administrator that assists with claims processing.
- A CPA firm whose accounting services to a healthcare provider involve access to PHI.
- An attorney whose legal services to a health plan involve access to PHI.
- A consultant who performs utilization reviews for a hospital.
- A healthcare clearinghouse that translates a claim from a non-standard format into a standard transaction on behalf of a healthcare provider, and forwards the processed transaction to a payer.
- An independent medical transcriptionist who provides transcription services to a physician.
- A pharmacy benefits manager who manages a health plan's pharmacist network.

Once a CE determines that an entity or an individual with which it has a business relationship meets the definition of a BA, the CE is responsible for ensuring that the third party complies with HIPAA. This is done with a contract or other agreement between the CE and BA. The contract, known as a business associate agreement (BAA), is a written arrangement that specifies each party's responsibilities with regard to PHI. (See Section 5.7.1 on BAAs.)

2.2.2.1 Identifying business associates

Managing the many relationships within a healthcare organization can be a daunting task, and determining which entities qualify as BAs is not always straightforward. It is important to examine each vendor relationship to determine whether a BA relationship exists and requires a written BAA.

There can be serious consequences for not identifying BAs or not formalizing the relationship with a BAA. Consider this case: In 2018, Pagosa Springs Medical Center (PSMC) agreed to pay $111,400 to settle an OCR investigation regarding potential HIPAA violations. The investigation revealed, among other things, that PSMC used Google to maintain its web-based scheduling calendar for patient appointments without signing a BAA with Google before the online company disclosed, stored, and saved PHI.[1]

My phone company or internet provider could access my patient information. Is a BAA needed?

No. Some entities that provide services to CEs are not considered BAs due to the nature of the service. In these cases, the entity merely acts as a conduit, transporting or transmitting PHI without actually accessing the information on a routine basis (other than infrequently)—such as the United States Postal Service, couriers and their electronic equivalents, and internet service providers. This is known as the conduit exception, which was defined as part of the Omnibus Final Rule in 2013. If the exception applies, there is no need for a BAA between the service provider and the CE.

In determining whether this fairly narrow exception applies, the CE must make a factual determination regarding the nature of the transmission services provided and the extent of PHI access. An important distinction to be made is whether the opportunity to access PHI is transient versus persistent—that is, whether the information is incidentally stored in order to perform transport/transmission of the information or if the information is actually, and deliberately stored by the entity. A vendor that transmits or transports PHI but also stores the PHI is not merely a conduit, and needs a BAA.

What about a landlord or cleaning service? They have access to the office where PHI is kept. Do I need a BAA with them?

No. You do not need to sign a BAA with a cleaning service, because the entity is not contracted to perform services involving the use or disclosure of PHI. However, you must have reasonable safeguards in place to protect PHI from people with access to your office, such as cleaning people and repair professionals. For example, all paper PHI should be kept safe in a locked cabinet, and any devices used for ePHI should have adequate protections.

---

[1] https://www.hhs.gov/about/news/2018/12/11/colorado-hospital-failed-to-terminate-former-employees-access-to-electronic-protected-health-information.html

Do I need to have a BAA with my accountant? She's been working with us for years, but isn't an employee.

Yes! CEs often overlook a BA who has been working with the organization for a long time. However, if an independent contractor is providing services, such as accounting or a similar service that involves access to PHI, you must have a BAA in place.

Ride-sharing companies: The latest HIPAA Business Associates

In March 2018 Uber introduced the launch of Uber Health, a new service that partners with healthcare organizations to provide transportation for their patients. Within days of the launch, Lyft and Allscripts announced a partnership to allow healthcare providers to schedule patient rides using Allscripts's electronic health record network.

Non-Emergency Medical Transportation services like Uber Health are an effort to eliminate transportation barriers for patients. According to a 2005 study, some 3.6 million people missed or delayed their medical appointments each year because they lacked transportation.

As ridesharing companies expand their services to the healthcare industry, HIPAA compliance has become an important consideration for those healthcare companies that partner with them. A CE that contracts with a ridesharing company to schedule transportation for patients and provides the company with the patient's name and home address for pick-up or drop-off is sharing PHI and creating a BA relationship. In this case, the healthcare provider must enter into a BAA with the ridesharing company before sharing PHI and offering these services to its patients.[2]

2.2.2.2 Exceptions to the BA standard

The Privacy Rule does not require CEs to have a BAA in place before PHI can be disclosed in these situations:

- Disclosures by a CE to a healthcare provider for treatment. For example:
    - A hospital does not need a BAA with a specialist to whom it refers a patient and transmits the patient's medical chart for treatment purposes.
    - A doctor does not need a BAA with a lab in order to disclose PHI to treat a patient.
    - A hospital lab does not need a BAA to disclose PHI to a reference laboratory to treat a patient.
- Disclosures by a CE to a health plan sponsor, such as an employer, by a group health plan, or by the health insurance issuer or HMO that provides health insurance benefits or coverage for the group health plan.

[2] https://1sthcc.com/ride-sharing-companies-are-your-new-hipaa-business-associates/

- Collecting and sharing PHI by a public benefits program, such as Medicare, and an agency other than the agency administering the health plan, such as the Social Security Administration.
- Disclosures by a healthcare provider to a health plan for payment, or when the healthcare provider accepts a discounted rate to participate in the health plan's network.
- With individuals or organizations whose services do not involve the use or disclosure of PHI and do not have more than incidental access to PHI.
- With a person or organization that is simply a conduit for PHI, such as the US Postal Service, some private couriers, and their electronic equivalents.
- Among CEs that participate in an organized healthcare arrangement (OHCA) to make disclosures that relate to the joint healthcare activities of the OHCA.
- Where a group health plan purchases insurance from a health insurance issuer or an HMO.
- Where a CE purchases a health plan product or other insurance, for example reinsurance, from an insurer.
- For research purposes, either with patient authorization or as a limited data set.
- When a financial institution processes financial transactions for healthcare or health plan premiums payment (unless functions that are above and beyond payment processing activities are performed, such as account receivable functions).

2.2.3 Hybrid entities

A hybrid entity is a single legal entity that performs both covered and non-covered functions, and that designates certain units as healthcare components. A hybrid entity must comply with HIPAA in some regards, but not others. If a CE opts not to hybridize, then it and all of its components are subject to HIPAA.

If a CE does decide to operate as a hybrid entity, it must clearly define and designate the healthcare component(s) that do and do not perform CE and/or BA functions, and document that

Hybrid entities don't escape HIPAA scrutiny

In 2016, the Office of Civil Rights (OCR) reached a settlement with the University of Massachusetts over the school's failure to designate certain counseling and occupational therapy centers that engaged in covered healthcare services as hybrid entity activities.

The settlement, which resulted in a fine of $650,000, concerned a malware attack that affected more than 1,500 records that included names, addresses, social security numbers and other personal identifiable information.

The OCR investigation found that the University did not follow all of the HIPAA hybrid entity requirements, did not take appropriate steps to secure PHI, and did not conduct the required risk analysis in a timely manner.[3]

[3] https://www.hhs.gov/hipaa/for-professionals/compliance-enforcement/agreements/umass/index.html

designation. For example, the research arm of a hybrid entity that functions as a healthcare provider and engages in standard electronic transactions would be subject to the Privacy Rule.

It is the entity's responsibility to decide whether it is a hybrid entity, and which of its components would be considered healthcare services. An entity should therefore carefully review its operations to determine which services and activities come under HIPAA.

2.2.4 Non-HIPAA covered entities

Not all companies with some type of contact or exposure to health information are required to comply with HIPAA. Below is a list of company types, organizations and agencies that are not required to follow HIPAA regulations:

- An employer that requests employee health information for sick leave or workers' compensation reasons. Note, however, that if the information is coming from a healthcare provider, the patient/employee must authorize the request.
- Non-healthcare-related government programs, such as the Supplemental Nutrition Assistance Program (SNAP)
- Insurance companies providing life insurance, long-term disability insurance, workers' compensation, auto insurance, property insurance or casualty insurance
- Most law enforcement agencies
- State agencies (for example, Child Protective Services)
- Search engines and mobile apps for health and fitness
- Health clubs/gyms
- Alternative medicine practitioners
- Most schools and school districts

2.3 Personal Representatives

A patient has the right to designate someone else to participate in their healthcare or to act on their behalf. These designated individuals are known as personal representatives, and have the same rights as the patient with regard to the patient's PHI. For example, a personal representative can request access to the person's PHI, request an accounting of disclosures (see Section 3.4), and can authorize PHI use or disclosure.

The personal representative may have broad authority to act on the patient's behalf, for example in the case of the parent of a minor or the legal guardian of a mentally incompetent adult, or the authority may be limited.

Personal Representatives

If the individual is:	The personal representative is:
An adult or an emancipated minor	A person with legal authority to make healthcare decisions on behalf of the individual *Examples:* Healthcare power of attorney Court-appointed legal guardian General power of attorney or durable power of attorney that includes the power to make healthcare decisions *Exceptions:* Abuse, neglect, and endangerment situations
An unemancipated minor	A parent, guardian, or other person acting in *loco parentis* with legal authority to make healthcare decisions on behalf of the minor child *Exceptions:* Exceptions to parents and unemancipated minors, and abuse, neglect, and endangerment situations
Deceased	A person with legal authority to act on behalf of the decedent or the estate (not restricted to persons with authority to make healthcare decisions) *Examples:* Executor or administrator of the estate Next of kin or other family member (if relevant law provides authority)

Source: https://www.hhs.gov/hipaa/for-professionals/privacy/guidance/personal-representatives/index.html

If the personal representative's authority is limited, the CE or BA must make sure it understands and observes the limits set by the patient. For example, if a personal representative is given permission to only authorize a specific treatment, such as artificial life support, the CE cannot ask the personal representative to authorize use or disclosure of the patient's PHI for marketing purposes.

If a personal representative is acting on behalf of a deceased person or their estate, the representative has the same rights that the patient would have with regard to PHI that is relevant to the representative's responsibilities to manage the deceased person's affairs. In this case, the CE does not have to specify healthcare decisions to provide the representative with the relevant PHI.

While parents are typically the personal representatives of unemancipated minors by default, there are three exceptions set out in the Privacy Rule that permit a minor to access certain healthcare without parental consent, and so do not give the parent access or control of the minor's PHI:

- When state or other law does not require parent or guardian consent, and the minor consents to the healthcare service, for example for mental health treatment.
- When someone other than the parent is authorized by law to act as the minor's personal representative, and gives consent. For example, a court may give another adult consent to act as a minor's representative, or the court itself may act as a minor's representative.
- When a parent agrees to a confidential relationship between the minor and a healthcare provider.

CEs and BAs should consult state law to check whether there are additional regulations regarding the authority of personal representatives. The Privacy Rule defers to state laws that expressly address a parent's right to access their offspring's medical information.

2.3.1 Situations of abuse, neglect, and endangerment

If a CE has reason to believe that an individual is the victim of domestic violence, abuse, or neglect by their personal representative, or believes that sharing medical information about a patient to a personal representative could result in harm to the patient, the CE can choose not to recognize the designated person as the patient's personal representative.

2.3.2 The privacy rights of deceased individuals

Under the Privacy Rule, the PHI of deceased individuals is protected for 50 years after the individual's death. This time period is designed to balance protecting the privacy of the deceased individual and the surviving relatives with the need to make the information available for historical purposes.

During the 50-year period, the deceased person's personal representative has the authority to authorize certain uses and disclosures of, and accessing, the decedent's PHI. The personal representative does not need to authorize PHI disclosures for someone who has been deceased for more than 50 years, and does not have rights to the deceased person's PHI.

CEs are also allowed to disclose relevant PHI to family members or others involved in the individual's healthcare or payment for care prior to the individual's death who are not personal representatives, unless the decedent made their wishes clear to restrict.

After 50 years have passed, a CE may use or disclose the information without regard to the Privacy Rule because the information is not considered protected health information.

2.4 Protected Health Information

2.4.1 PHI

Under the HIPAA Privacy Rule, PHI is defined as individually identifiable health information (IIHI) held or transmitted by a CE or BA in any form or media, including electronic, paper and oral, that identifies the patient or could reasonably be used to identify the patient, and relates to the following:

- A patient's past, present, or future physical or mental health condition
- All healthcare provided to the patient
- Past, present, or future payments for treatment provided to the patient

PHI is typically found in medical forms, documents, and communications, such as laboratory reports, radiology reports, and hospital bills.

Types of PHI data include the following 18 identifiers of the individual or of relatives, employers, or household members of the individual if it is associated with health information:

- Name
- Addresses: In particular, anything more specific than the state, including street address, city, county, precinct, and in most cases zip code, and their equivalent geocodes
- Telephone number
- Fax number
- Email address
- Dates (except for year): date of birth, date of death, date of service, date of admittance, date of discharge
- Social security number

- Medical record numbers
- Account numbers
- Health plan beneficiary numbers
- Certification/license numbers
- Vehicle identifiers and serial numbers, including license plate numbers
- Device identifiers and serial numbers
- Internet Protocol (IP) addresses
- Web Universal Resource Locations (URLs)
- Biometric identifier (fingerprint/voiceprint)
- Full-face photographic image
- Other unique identifying numbers, characteristics or codes

Is it PHI?

When you are determining whether information should be considered PHI, the relationship of the information with medical circumstances is key. Identifying information alone that is not related to treatment or payment, such as personal names, residential addresses, or phone numbers, would not necessarily be designated as PHI.

In the wrong hands, any of these data types could be used to identify somebody and link them to their private medical information.

2.4.1.1 ePHI

Electronic protected health information (ePHI) refers to the subset of any PHI covered by HIPAA that is produced, saved, transmitted or received in electronic form. ePHI is specifically addressed by the HIPAA Security Rule (See Chapter 5).

2.4.2 Non-PHI

Not all individual identifiable information is considered PHI. For example, a CE's employment records, or student health information in education records that are protected by the Family Educational Rights and Privacy Act (FERPA) are not considered PHI because the information is not linked to health records that could compromise an individual's medical privacy.

In addition, some health information isn't considered PHI because it can't be used to identify an individual, or because it is not created, received, maintained, or transmitted by a CE or BA.

Examples include:

- Number of steps from a pedometer
- Number of calories burned
- Blood sugar readings without personally identifiable user information (such as an account or user name)

- Heart rate readings without PHI
- Average age of health plan members (the aggregated information does not identify individual members)

2.4.3 De-identified PHI

De-identified patient data is information that cannot be used to link an individual to healthcare situations. There are no privacy restrictions on de-identified health information, and it is considered a valuable asset to the healthcare community because it can be used to improve care, estimate the costs of care, and support public health initiatives.

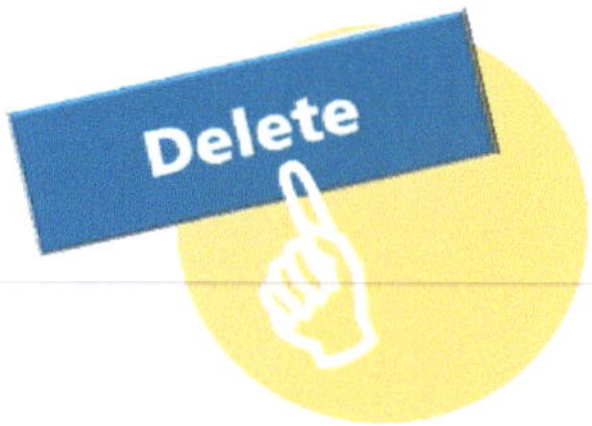

De-identified PHI is a medical record that has had all "direct identifiers" such as those listed in Section 2.4.1, to the point where the patient can't be recognized.

There are several accepted methods for de-identifying PHI in order to use it for studies, cost analysis, etc. For example, a qualified statistician could wipe data clean and declare PHI unrecognizable; or, a CE could remove the 18 direct identifiers that constitute PHI data and stipulate that, to the best of its knowledge, the data could not be used alone or in combination with other information to determine a patient's identity.

2.4.4 Psychotherapy notes

Psychotherapy notes are a subset of PHI that receive special consideration under HIPAA, because they may contain personal notes and sensitive information that is not needed for treatment, payment, or healthcare operations.

Psychotherapy notes receive special consideration under HIPAA.

Psychotherapy notes refer to any notes taken by a mental health professional while providing mental health treatment, such as private, group, joint, or family counseling. The notes are kept separate from the rest of the patient's medical record and are not typically disclosed for other purposes.

Under the Privacy Rule, psychotherapy notes are specifically excluded from a patient's general right to access or inspect their own medical records (see Section 3.1). In other words, mental health professionals can refuse to provide patients with access to their own psychotherapy notes.

CEs must get specific authorization from a patient before psychotherapy notes can be disclosed to a third party. The patient's request must be recorded on a form used exclusively to document the authorization to release psychotherapy notes.

Psychotherapy notes do not include PHI kept elsewhere in the medical record, nor the following:

- Medication prescription and monitoring
- Counseling session start and stop times
- Types and frequencies of treatment provided
- Results of clinical tests
- Any summary of the following items: Diagnosis, functional status, treatment plan, symptoms, prognosis, patient progress

2.5 Permitted Uses and Disclosures of PHI

HIPAA protects an individual's right to keep PHI private and confidential. However, there are a variety of reasons that healthcare providers need to use and share PHI, such as communicating with insurance companies to expedite payment, or sharing PHI among healthcare providers for patient care. Effectively sharing this information is an essential and critical component of providing healthcare.

This is a key reason HIPAA exists: In addition to requiring that CEs take measures to keep PHI private and confidential, HIPAA was designed to articulate and regulate the reasons that PHI can be used, shared, or disclosed.

In the broadest sense, PHI can be disclosed for one of two reasons:

1. The patient gives permission.
2. HIPAA allows (or requires) the disclosure.

It's important to understand the difference between the two in order to effectively safeguard and also effectively use and disclose PHI.

2.5.1 The patient gives permission

Patients can give written authorization or consent for use and disclosure of their PHI. Although the words may sound synonymous, there are differences between the two under HIPAA.

2.5.1.1 Consent

CEs need to use and share PHI in order to provide healthcare and receive payment. Individuals expect that their health information will be used as necessary for treatment, billing for that treatment, and, to some extent, to operate the healthcare business. Therefore, the Privacy Rule does not require CEs to obtain a patient's authorization for treatment, payment, and healthcare operations (TPO). CEs may choose to obtain consent for TPO functions, and if so, they can decide how to obtain consent and what to include on a patient consent form.

Patient consent for use and disclosure of PHI for TPO functions cannot be applied to any other uses or disclosures that specifically require written authorization under HIPAA.

2.5.1.2 Authorization

Patient authorization is a detailed document that provides CEs with explicit permission to use and disclose PHI for purposes other than TPO.

As a general rule, CEs need to obtain a valid patient authorization before using and disclosing PHI for any reason that is not covered by the required or permitted uses and disclosures under the Privacy Rule. Relying only on a patient's consent, even if they have signed a consent form, when an authorization is required by the Privacy Rule is an unauthorized use of PHI.

There are three situations that explicitly require authorization:

- **Psychotherapy notes.** A CE is required to get patient authorization for use or disclosure of psychotherapy notes, except for these situations: the notes are being used by the healthcare professional who generated them; the CE uses the notes to for mental healthcare training; the CE uses the notes to defend itself in a lawsuit brought against it by the patient; or, the use or disclosure is required by the Privacy Rule. (See Section 2.5.2.)
- **Marketing activities.** The CE must get written authorization from a patient to use or disclose PHI for marketing efforts, unless the marketing communication was made directly by the CE to the patient or the communication is in the form of a gift of nominal value from the CE.

Examine all marketing activities through a HIPAA lens

Before an orthodontist posts before and after pictures of patients on Instagram, she needs to consider HIPAA regulations.

Patient photos and testimonials can provide compelling marketing narratives, but they can also expose CEs to complaints of unauthorized PHI disclosure. Marketing activities should be shared with the compliance officer, and HIPAA training should be provided to workforce members who may want to access PHI for marketing and social media efforts.

Consider this case: A California physical therapy practice agreed to pay $25,000 for sharing patient testimonials without permission. In 2012, a patient filed a complaint against Complete P.T., Pool & Physical Therapy (CPT), claiming that the practice had posted patient testimonials on its website without patient authorization. The online testimonials included patient names and photographs. An OCR investigation found that CPT had disclosed PHI without permission. During the investigation, OCR also discovered that the organization did not have reasonable safeguards to protect patient privacy or effective policies and procedures to obtain authorization to disclose PHI.[4]

Appendix B of this book includes a sample social media policy that can be used as a reference to develop and implement policies and procedures.

- **Sale of PHI.** The CE is required to get authorization from patients if it plans to sell patient PHI. On the authorization form, the CE must plainly state that it intends to sell the PHI for money.

It is important to note that a CE cannot require a patient to sign an authorization as a prerequisite for treatment.

Sections 2.7.2 and 2.7.3 discuss valid and invalid authorizations in detail.

Employers need HIPAA authorization

HIPAA does not apply to employment records that contain health-related information, even if the employer is considered a CE or BA. However, as a general rule, the employer will need to obtain a HIPAA Authorization from the employee if it needs to obtain medical information from the employee's healthcare provider. In this way, HIPAA impacts employers when handling FMLA, ADA, drug test results, and other medical benefits for employees.

[4] https://www.hhs.gov/sites/default/files/cpt-res-agreement.pdf

2.5.2 HIPAA allows or requires the disclosure

HIPAA allows CEs to use their professional ethics and best judgment to share PHI without obtaining patient authorization in certain situations that are clearly defined by the rule. Six of those situations *allow* the CE to use or disclose the information, and two of those situations *require* the CE to use or disclose the information:

Permitted disclosures:

1. The disclosure is made to the patient.
2. The disclosure is for treatment, payment, or healthcare operations.
3. The patient is given the opportunity to agree or object to the use or disclosure.
4. The use or disclosure is considered incidental.
5. The use or disclosure for public interest or benefit activities.
6. The use or disclosure is a limited data set for research, public health, or healthcare operations.

Required disclosures:

1. A CE is required to disclose PHI if a patient requests access to their PHI, or requests an accounting of disclosures of their PHI (See Section 3.4 for patient access).
2. A CE is required to disclose PHI to HHS for the purposes of a compliance investigation, review, or enforcement action. (See Chapter 7 for Enforcement.)

2.5.2.1 Permitted Disclosures

2.5.2.1.1 The disclosure is made to the patient

Under HIPAA, patients have the right to access their information. Therefore, the CE can disclose PHI directly to the patient or the patient's personal representative (see Section 2.3) without an authorization.

Caregivers can share confidential medical information with their patients without an authorization.

2.5.2.1.2 The disclosure is for treatment, payment, or healthcare operations

A CE is permitted to use and disclose PHI for TPO activities without an authorization. When using or disclosing the PHI for these activities, both the disclosing CE and the receiving CE are required to follow all HIPAA privacy requirements. The disclosing CE is responsible for the PHI right up until the receiving CE has received the information. The disclosing CE is required to use or disclose the PHI in a "permitted and secure" manner, which includes complying with HIPAA Privacy and Security safeguards when sending the PHI, and taking reasonable steps to make sure the PHI is going to the correct address and to the correct person or department.

Once the receiving CE takes possession of the PHI, it is responsible for keeping the PHI private and secure, including with respect to subsequent uses or disclosures, or any breaches that occur.

2.5.2.1.2.1 Uses and disclosures for treatment

HIPAA permits healthcare providers to share PHI to treat or coordinate patient care. CEs may disclose PHI orally, on paper, by fax, or electronically to another provider for treatment activities without patient authorization.

Treatment is broadly defined to include:

- The provision, coordination, or management of healthcare and related services by one or more providers, including the coordination or management of healthcare by a provider with a third party.
- Consultation between providers regarding a patient.
- A patient referral for care from one provider to another.

Examples of treatment include: a primary care provider who sends a copy of her patient's medical record to a specialist; or a hospital nurse sending a patient's healthcare instructions to a nursing home where the patient has been transferred for rehabilitative care.

Is a patient's authorization required before providing patient information to a pharmacy for filling a prescription?

No. Under the HIPAA Privacy Rule, a healthcare provider can exchange PHI for treatment, payment, or operations. Providing information to a patient's chosen pharmacy for treatment purposes would fall under this exception, so patient authorization is not required.

2.5.2.1.2.2 Uses and disclosures for payment

Payment refers to the activities that healthcare providers use to obtain payment or be reimbursed for their services, and the activities that health plans use to obtain premiums, to fulfill their coverage responsibilities, and provide benefits under the plan, as well as to obtain or provide reimbursement for providing healthcare. The Privacy Rule provides some examples of common payment activities, which include (but are not limited to):

- Determining eligibility or coverage under a plan and adjudicating claims
- Risk adjustments
- Billing and collection
- Reviewing healthcare services for medical necessity, coverage, and justification of charges
- Utilization review
- Disclosures to consumer reporting agencies (limited to specified identifying information about the individual, their payment history, and identifying information about the CE)

Examples of allowed uses and disclosures for payment include: a doctor sending a patient's health insurance information to a lab because the lab will need to bill the patient's insurance for tests; or, a hospital ER giving a patient's payment information to an ambulance company so that the company can bill the patient for the transport service.

2.5.2.1.2.3 Uses and disclosures for healthcare operations

Covered entities need to share PHI to run their businesses and provide care.

Healthcare operations are the business activities that a CE engages in to provide healthcare services and obtain payment. Operations include administrative, financial, legal, and quality improvement activities that are related to covered services.

A CE can disclose PHI to another CE or to a BA orally, on paper, by fax, or electronically for the following healthcare operations activities without patient authorization:

- Conducting quality assessment and improvement activities
- Developing clinical guidelines
- Conducting patient safety activities, as defined in applicable regulations
- Conducting population-based activities relating to improving health or reducing healthcare cost

- Developing protocols
- Conducting case management and care coordination (including care planning)
- Contacting healthcare providers and patients with information about treatment alternatives
- Reviewing the qualifications of healthcare professionals
- Evaluating performance of healthcare providers and/or health plans
- Conducting training programs or credentialing activities
- Supporting fraud and abuse detection and compliance programs

A CE is required to meet the following **three** conditions when using or disclosing PHI for operations activities:

1. Both CEs must have or have had a relationship with the patient (it can be a past or present patient);
2. The PHI requested must be regarding the relationship; and
3. The discloser must disclose only the "minimum information necessary" for the specified healthcare operation. (See Section 2.6.)

2.5.2.1.3 Uses and disclosures with an opportunity to agree or object

The Privacy Rule permits CEs to use or disclose PHI without obtaining an authorization for certain limited purposes if the individual is given the opportunity to agree or object. These purposes include: using patient information facility directories; using or disclosing PHI for involvement in the individual's care; and, using or disclosing PHI for notification purposes.

The CE can ask the individual for permission, or permission can happen by circumstances that clearly give the individual the opportunity to agree or object. If the individual is incapacitated, in an emergency situation, or not available, CEs generally may use or disclose PHI, if they believe it is in the best interests of the individual.

2.5.2.1.3.1 Facility directories

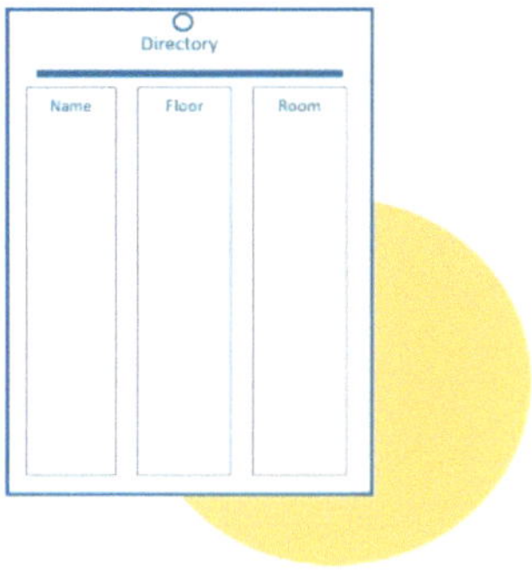

Some healthcare facilities (for example hospitals) maintain patient directories. CEs are permitted to list certain patient information in these directories, such as names, general condition, religious affiliation, and room numbers. However, the CE must tell the patient about the directory and the information that will be included, and also explain to the patient who will have access to the directory. The patient must be given the chance to restrict the personal information included in the directory, who has access to that information, and to opt out of being included altogether.

The CE can disclose the individual's condition and location to anyone who asks for the individual by name (such as a visitor), and can also disclose religious affiliation to clergy. Clergy do not have to ask for individuals by name when inquiring about patients' religious affiliation.

2.5.2.1.3.2 For notification and other purposes

A CE is permitted to disclose PHI to a patient's family, relatives, or friends, (or even other people that the patient identifies) in these situations:

- The patient gives permission.
- The patient doesn't object.
- The friends or relatives are involved in caring for the patient or paying for treatment.
- The CE uses its professional judgment, believing that disclosing the information is in the patient's best interests, and believes the patient has no objections, for example, if the patient is not present or is unconscious.

Sharing PHI with a patient's family and friends

- An emergency room doctor may discuss treatment in front of a friend if the patient asks the friend to come into the treatment room.
- A nurse may inform a patient that they are going to tell a relative how the patient is doing, and proceed to do so as long as the patient does not object. The nurse may not discuss the patient's condition with relatives if the patient does not give consent.
- A hospital may discuss a patient's bill with the patient's daughter who is at the hospital and has questions about the charges.
- A doctor may talk to a relative who is driving a patient home from the hospital about keeping the patient's foot elevated during the ride home.
- A doctor may discuss a patient's medication with a health aide who accompanies the patient to an appointment.

For example, a pharmacist can give a filled prescription to a patient's relative, or a surgeon can provide a spouse with information about the procedure while the patient is still unconscious.

Note however, that only information that is relevant to the care at that moment can be shared with others. A caregiver cannot share past medical issues with friends or family if the problems are not directly related to the present issue.

A CE is also permitted to use or disclose PHI to identify, locate, and notify family members or others involved in the patient's care of the individual's location, general condition, or death. PHI can also be disclosed to public or private entities authorized to assist in disaster relief efforts.

2.5.2.1.4 Incidental use and disclosure

The Privacy Rule is not intended to hermetically seal off the flow of medical information. Patients and caregivers depend on the efficient exchange of PHI to manage healthcare and expedite payment.

The Privacy Rule recognizes that this information exchange will occasionally result in "incidental" PHI disclosure, and does not require CEs to eliminate every risk of incidental use or disclosure. In other words, if PHI is used or disclosed as a result of, or as "incident to," an otherwise permitted use or disclosure, it is not considered a violation of the Privacy Rule, so long as the CE has set up reasonable technical and physical safeguards to protect the privacy of the PHI, and the information being shared was limited to the "minimum necessary" (see Section 2.6) as required by the Privacy Rule.

HHS offers these examples of incidental use: A hospital visitor overhears a physician's confidential conversation with another physician; or, a visitor sees patient information on a nursing station whiteboard or on a sign-in sheet.

The Rule does **not** permit incidental uses or disclosures if they are the result of a Privacy Rule violation.

2.5.2.1.5 Public interest and benefit activities

CEs are permitted to use and disclose PHI without an individual's authorization for 12 national priority purposes. These disclosures are not required, but the Privacy Rule allows them for public interest. Note that the Rule puts limitations on each purpose to balance the need for individual privacy and the public's need for the information.

The twelve activities are:

1. Disclosures required by law, including by statute, regulation, or court orders.

2. Disclosures supporting public health activities. CEs can disclose to:

   a. Public health authorities in order to prevent or control disease, injury, or disability; and to agencies authorized to receive reports of child abuse and neglect.

   b. Entities subject to regulation from the Food and Drug Administration (FDA) regarding FDA-regulated products or activities for purposes such as adverse event reporting, tracking of products, product recalls, and post-marketing surveillance.

   c. Individuals who may have contracted or been exposed to a communicable disease (when notification is authorized by law).

   d. Employers, regarding employees (when requested by employers) for information concerning a work-related illness or injury or workplace-related medical surveillance, when the information is needed to comply with the Occupational Safety and Health Administration (OSHA), the Mine Safety and Health Administration (MHSA), or a similar state law.

3. Disclosures to government authorities related to abuse, neglect, or domestic violence.

4. Disclosures for health oversight activities such as audits and investigations necessary for oversight of the healthcare system and government benefit programs.

5. Disclosures for judicial and administrative proceedings if CE receives a PHI request through a court order, administrative tribunal, in response to a subpoena or other lawful process. In some circumstances, the CE may require assurances that a notice to the individual or a protective order will be provided.

6. Disclosures for law enforcement purposes. The Rule identifies six circumstances where a CE can disclose PHI, subject to specified conditions:

   a. As required by law (including court orders, court-ordered warrants, subpoenas) and administrative requests;

   b. To identify or locate a suspect, fugitive, material witness, or missing person;

   c. In response to a law enforcement official's request for information about a victim or suspected victim of a crime;

   d. To alert law enforcement of a person's death, if the CE believes that the death is the result of criminal activity;

   e. When a CE believes PHI is evidence of a crime that occurred on its premises; or,

   f. To inform law enforcement about a crime, its victims, or a perpetrator in a medical emergency not occurring on its premises.

7. Disclosures for activities related to a death, including providing PHI to funeral directors, and to coroners or medical examiners to identify a deceased person, determine the cause of death, and perform other functions authorized by law.
8. Disclosures to facilitate organ, eye, or tissue donation from a cadaver.
9. Disclosures for research. A CE can use and disclose PHI for research purposes if it obtains:
   a. Documentation that an alteration or waiver of individuals' authorization for the use or disclosure of PHI for research purposes has been approved by an Institutional Review Board or Privacy Board;
   b. Assurances from the researcher that the PHI will only be used to prepare a research protocol, that the researcher will not remove any PHI from the CE, and that the PHI is essential for the research; or,

   c. Assurances from the researcher that only the PHI of deceased individuals will be used, that the PHI is necessary for the research, and, at the request of the CE, documentation of the death of the individuals about whom information is sought.
10. Disclosures related to serious threats to health or safety, to prevent or lessen a serious and imminent threat to a person or the public. A CE may also disclose PHI to law enforcement if the information is needed to identify or apprehend an escapee or violent criminal.
11. Disclosures that are essential to government functions, such as a military mission, conducting intelligence and national security activities authorized by law, protecting the President, making medical suitability determinations for U.S. State Department employees, protecting the health and safety of inmates or employees in a prison, and determining eligibility for or conducting enrollment in certain government benefit programs.
12. Disclosures related to workers' compensation.

Tarasoff, Aurora, Newtown: Protecting the patient and public from harm

In the wake of the mass shootings that occurred in Aurora, CO and Newtown, CT in 2012, the OCR issued a letter in January 2013 that provided guidance for healthcare providers regarding the ability to disclose information about a patient to law enforcement or others to protect the patient or the public from harm.

The duty to warn has its roots in the 1974 CA Supreme Court decision *Tarasoff v. the Regents of the University of California*,[5] which established a duty of healthcare providers to share warnings about credible threats of violence.

That duty was reaffirmed in the 2013 OCR letter,[6] which sought to balance patient privacy concerns with public health and safety:

> When a healthcare provider believes in good faith that such a warning is necessary to prevent or lessen a serious and imminent threat to the health or safety of the patient or others, the Privacy Rule allows the provider, consistent with applicable law and standards of ethical conduct, to alert those persons whom the provider believes are reasonably able to prevent or lessen the threat.
>
> Under these provisions, a healthcare provider may disclose patient information, including information from mental health records, if necessary, to law enforcement, family members of the patient, or any other persons who may reasonably be able to prevent or lessen the risk of harm.

The letter noted that most states have laws and/or court decisions supporting—even requiring—the disclosure of protected information in the interest of public safety, and recommends that healthcare providers consult state law as well as federal law governing the disclosure of substance abuse treatment records.

2.5.2.1.5.1 Privacy and the Subpoena

CEs should understand their obligations and liabilities under the law and exercise due diligence when responding to a subpoena for medical records.

Subpoenas are routinely used by attorneys to obtain medical records from third parties for a variety of civil lawsuits ranging from personal injury to employment law to medical malpractice claims. The CE must take specific measures to protect a patient's right to privacy when responding to subpoenas. Under HIPAA, a CE may disclose PHI without a written authorization from the patient pursuant to a subpoena that satisfies **one** of these conditions:

1. The attorney must provide the CE a written statement demonstrating that:
   a. A good faith attempt was made to provide written notice of the subpoena to the patient or his or her attorney;

---

[5] *Tarasoff v. Regents of the University of California*, 551 P.2d 334 (Cal. 1976).

[6] https://www.hhs.gov/sites/default/files/ocr/office/lettertonationhcp.pdf

   b. The written notice included sufficient information to allow the patient to raise an objection to the subpoena;
   c. The time for objecting to the subpoena has passed; or
   d. The patient did not object to the subpoena, or any objections by the patient were adequately resolved by the court.
2. The attorney must provide the CE a written statement stating all parties to the lawsuit have agreed to a qualified protective order. A qualified protective order limits the use of the requested PHI to the lawsuit and requires the PHI to be returned or destroyed when the lawsuit ends.
3. The CE makes reasonable efforts to provide notice of the subpoena to the patient and the patient does not object to the PHI release.
4. The CE obtains a signed HIPAA authorization from the patient to release the subpoenaed PHI.

Upon receiving a subpoena, a CE should:

1. Take note of when the documents must be produced or inspected;
2. Request a time extension if the deadline does not seem feasible (make sure to document the request and approval in writing); and,
3. Review the subpoena against the HIPAA-required documentation. If the information contained in the subpoena does not meet one of the listed HIPAA conditions, the CE must obtain the necessary documentation from the attorney in a timely manner, or contact the patient directly to obtain authorization.

The subpoena, accompanying documentation, and any written correspondences between the CE and attorney should be retained in case of an investigation or audit.

Once the CE confirms the subpoena is valid, it must release the medical records on the specified date. If the issuing attorney cannot produce the documentation, or if the patient does not allow the CE to make the disclosure, then the CE is simply not authorized to disclose the subpoenaed medical records. In this case, the CE should immediately contact an attorney, as it will need to object to the subpoena in writing, detailing the reasons for its objections, including the documentation needed to comply with HIPAA.

Who issued the subpoena?

Despite its legal language, a subpoena signed by an attorney or a court clerk differs from a court order or subpoena signed by a judicial officer, for example a judge or a magistrate. This distinction is important because of the exceptions carved out by HIPAA. If a CE receives a court order or subpoena signed by a judge or magistrate, a court-ordered warrant, or grand jury subpoena, it must disclose the requested documents. The CE must still pay careful attention not to disclose more than what is expressly authorized by the document to stay HIPAA-compliant. On the other hand, the CE must take the steps mentioned above if presented with a subpoena signed by anyone other than a judge or magistrate.

2.5.2.1.6 Limited data set for the purposes of research, public health or healthcare operations

A limited data set is partially de-identified PHI that can be used for research, healthcare operations, and public health purposes, so long as the recipient of the PHI enters into a data use agreement promising specified safeguards for the PHI within the limited data set.

2.5.2.2 Required Disclosures

A CE is required to disclose PHI if a patient requests access to their PHI, or an accounting of disclosures of their PHI. (See Section 3.4.)

A CE is required to disclose PHI to HHS for the purposes of a compliance investigation, review, or enforcement action. (See Chapter 7.)

2.6 Minimum Necessary Standard

According to the HIPAA Privacy Rule, CEs cannot simply make any and all information available when using or disclosing PHI. The Privacy Rule exists to ensure that any PHI accessed by staff, shared, disclosed, or requested from another CE or BA is done in a mindful manner that protects the patient and safeguards confidentiality. This concept, known as the "minimum necessary standard," is a key protection of the Privacy Rule.

According to the standard, CEs are required to limit the use or disclosure of PHI to the minimum amount necessary to accomplish the intended purpose.

In the CE workplace, the standard means that workforce members who do not need to see patient PHI to do their jobs should not have access to it. It means that when a CE shares PHI with another CE or a BA, it only shares the information needed for that particular purpose.

Only those workforce members who need access to PHI to do their jobs should have access, and access should be limited to the minimum necessary to do that job.

For example, an entire patient history should not be shared to expedite payment for a specific treatment.

When implementing the minimum necessary standard, CEs are required to evaluate their practices to limit unnecessary or inappropriate access to PHI by determining which workforce members need access to PHI and under what conditions, based on job responsibilities and the nature of the business.

For example, a hospital may have rules that permit caregivers to access patients' entire medical record to expedite treatment. If so, the hospital's policies and procedures must specify that this level of access is allowed, and include a justification explaining why all of the entity's caregivers need complete access to medical records. It is unlikely, however, that *all* of the hospital's employees (including administrative and other non-caregiver staff) need routine, unlimited access to patients' medical records in order to do their jobs. If a hospital allows unrestricted access, it is not properly applying the minimum necessary standard. If an unauthorized use or disclosure were to result from this practice, it would be considered a violation of the Privacy Rule.

CEs can apply standard protocols to limit PHI to the minimum necessary for routine or recurring requests and disclosures, rather than reviewing each use or disclosure individually. Non-routine disclosures and requests must be reviewed on a case-by-case basis, and the CE must develop reasonable criteria to meet the minimum necessary standard.

There are exceptions to the minimum necessary standard. It does not apply in the following situations:

- Disclosures to or requests by a healthcare provider for treatment purposes.
- Disclosures to the individual who is the subject of the information.
- Uses or disclosures authorized by the individual.
- Uses or disclosures required for HIPAA compliance.
- Disclosures to HHS when required for enforcement purposes.
- Uses or disclosures required by other laws, such as state laws.

2.6.1 Reasonable reliance

The Privacy Rule allows a CE to rely on the judgment of the person or entity requesting the PHI disclosure to determine the minimum amount of information needed. This is permitted when the request is made by:

- A public official or agency that specifies that the information requested is the minimum necessary for a purpose permitted under the Privacy Rule, such as for public health purposes;
- Another CE;
- A staff member or BA of the CE who confirms that the information requested is the minimum necessary for the stated purpose; or

- A researcher with appropriate documentation from an institutional review board or privacy board.

Important reminders regarding permitted uses and disclosures

- CEs must address permitted uses and disclosures in their Notice of Privacy Practices.
- CEs must follow minimum necessary policies and procedures and apply reasonable Privacy Rule administrative, technical, and physical safeguards.

2.7 PHI Practices

HIPAA requires CEs to comply with certain practices to ensure that patients are aware of how PHI can be used and disclosed, and to seek patient authorization when necessary.

2.7.1 Notice of privacy practices

A notice of privacy practices (NPP) is a statement that describes how the CE may use and disclose a patient's medical information, and the practices that the CE has implemented to keep PHI private. It also explains how patients can access their information and exercise their rights under HIPAA.

CEs are required by the Privacy Rule to draft an NPP in "plain language" and make it available to patients. The NPP must include the following information:

1. **A header.** The NPP must contain a header or a prominently displayed box containing this statement: "This Notice describes how medical information about you may be used and disclosed, and how you can get access to this information. Please review it carefully."
2. **How the CE may use and disclose PHI.** This section lists, with examples, all of the ways that the CE is permitted by HIPAA to use and disclose the patient's PHI.
3. **Uses and disclosures for additional activities.** If the CE uses PHI for fundraising, if it releases PHI to group health plan sponsors, or it uses PHI for underwriting purposes, it must include a statement describing those activities in a separate statement. With regard to underwriting, it must include language that says the CE is prohibited from using an individual's genetic PHI for this purpose. With regard to fundraising, it must inform the individual of the right to opt out of receiving such communications.

4. **The individual's rights with regard to PHI**:
    a. The right to request disclosure restrictions. The NPP should also include a statement that says the CE is not required to agree to requested restrictions, unless the patient pays for the services in full.
    b. The right to receive PHI through confidential communication.
    c. The right to request access.
    d. The right to request an amendment to the medical record.
    e. The right to request an accounting of disclosures.
    f. The right to request a paper copy of the NPP.
5. **The CE's legal duties** with respect to the information, including statements that:
    a. The CE is required by law to maintain the privacy of PHI.
    b. The CE must notify patient impacted by a breach of unsecured PHI.
    c. The CE reserves the right to change the terms of its NPP and explain how notice of the change will be provided to patients.
6. **The individual's right to file a HIPAA complaint with the CE or the Secretary of HHS**, with instructions for filing the complaint, and a statement of non-retaliation.
7. **Contact information** for individual (name or title and telephone number) who can provide further information about the CE's privacy policies.
8. **The effective date of the NPP**, which cannot be retroactive.

A CE that has a direct treatment relationship with a patient must provide a copy of the NPP on the patient's first visit and make a good-faith effort to obtain a written acknowledgment of receipt from the patient. (A sample NPP Acknowledgment can be found in Appendix B of this book.)

NPP Templates

HHS has developed sets of model NPPs that health plans and healthcare providers can tailor and use for their operations. Each set contains three formatted options and a text-only option, in both English and Spanish:

https://www.hhs.gov/hipaa/for-professionals/privacy/guidance/model-notices-privacy-practices/index.html

In addition, the CE should make its NPP available to anyone who asks for it and post it prominently at its facility.

CEs that maintain a website with information about customer services or benefits must also post the NPP on the website.

The CE must promptly revise its NPP whenever it makes a change to its privacy practices, and must make patients aware of the changes by having copies available for patients to request and take with them, posting it in a prominent location at the facility, and on its website if it has one.

Are hospitals or other healthcare providers required to provide an NPP to patients they treat in an emergency?

No. A CE with a direct treatment relationship with an individual is not required to provide an NPP to a patient at the time of emergency treatment. In these situations, the HIPAA Privacy Rule requires only that providers give patients an NPP when it is practical to do so, after the emergency situation has ended.

The Privacy Rule also does not require that providers make a good-faith effort to obtain the patient's written acknowledgment of receipt of the notice if providing the NPP is delayed by an emergency treatment situation.

2.7.1.1 NPP options for organizations

A CE is encouraged to develop multiple NPPs if it performs different types of covered functions and the privacy practices vary for the different functions. The CE should then provide the most specific NPP available.

CEs that participate in an organized healthcare arrangement with other CEs can opt to use a single, joint NPP, as long as certain requirements are met. For example, the joint NPP must list and describe the CEs and describe the service delivery sites covered by the notice.

When any of the participating CEs provides the joint NPP to an individual, the NPP distribution requirement is automatically met for the other participating CEs.

2.7.1.1.2 NPPs for group health plans

Health plans must also provide plan participants with an NPP. The notice must be provided to participants no later than the compliance date for the health plan, and to any new participants who join the plan after the initial enrollment, for example, new employees who enroll in their employers' benefits plan. A health plan with multiple NPPs only has to send the NPP that is relevant to a given participant.

The health plan must notify participants covered by the plan that an NPP is available, and must explain how to obtain one. This notification must be done at least every three years. It is sufficient to notify the policyholder (dependents do not need to be notified separately.)

If the health plan makes the NPP available on its website, it must post notice of any changes or revisions to the NPP on the website where it is easy to see, including the effective date of change and how to get a copy of the revised NPP. The revised NPP or information about the revision should be included in the health plan's next annual mailing to plan participants.

Health plans that do not make NPPs available on their website must provide participants with a revised NPP or information about the changes and how to obtain a copy of the notice to all plan participants within 60 days of the changes.

A group health plan that only provides health benefits through an insurance contract and does not create or receive PHI other than summary health information or information about the individual's participation in the plan is not required to maintain or provide an NPP.

Must a CE with an NPP that reflects more stringent state laws of multiple states revise the whole notice every time one state law materially changes?

Perhaps. If a CE's NPP reflects the more stringent state laws of multiple states, it must be updated whenever a material change occurs in the state law of any state covered in the NPP. The CE must let individuals know that the NPP has been revised within 60 days of the revision.

However, a CE could choose to use an NPP that has a general statement in the uses and disclosures section that refers the reader to a separate section of the Notice containing the more stringent state privacy law(s). In the event of a change to state privacy laws affecting the CE, the CE would only need to revise the section of the NPP that contains the state-law-specific information.

This would also allow the CE to insert the revised state law section into existing NPP, rather than creating a new one.

2.7.1.2 NPP acknowledgment of receipt

An acknowledgment of receipt is the form that patients are asked to sign on the first visit to acknowledge that they have received a copy of the NPP.

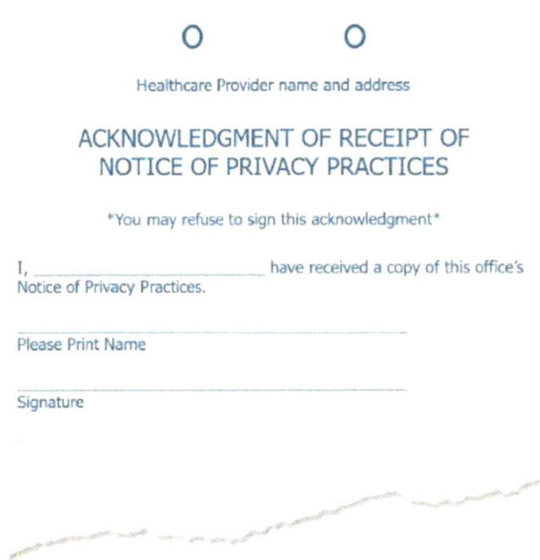
Healthcare Provider name and address

ACKNOWLEDGMENT OF RECEIPT OF NOTICE OF PRIVACY PRACTICES

You may refuse to sign this acknowledgment

I, ______________ have received a copy of this office's Notice of Privacy Practices.

____
Please Print Name

____
Signature

A CE with a direct treatment relationship with individuals is required to make a good-faith effort to obtain an individual's acknowledgement of receipt when the provider first gives the notice to the individual — that is, the first time that service is provided. An acknowledgment of receipt does not need to be signed by the patient each time.

What should a CE do if a patient refuses to sign an acknowledgment of receipt? The CE must try to get the patient to sign the receipt (and take the time to explain to the patient how the NPP works), but if an individual refuses to sign, the CE cannot compel them to sign, and cannot refuse to treat the patient simply because they have not signed the acknowledgment of receipt.

In addition, a patient's refusal to sign does **not** free the provider from complying with its privacy obligations. Staff should document efforts to obtain the patient's signature on the acknowledgment, and the reason why the acknowledgment was not signed.

A patient's first visit

Patients should receive a copy of the NPP on their first visit, and should be asked to sign an acknowledgment of receipt. The signed acknowledgment (or a note documenting a patient's refusal to sign the acknowledgment) should be placed in the patient's medical records.

2.7.2 Authorization to release PHI

When the Privacy Rule requires written patient authorization for a use or disclosure of PHI, a general patient consent is not sufficient. The CE must obtain written authorization from the patient for the PHI use or disclosure.

The authorization is a detailed document that gives the CE permission to use the PHI for the specified purposes. It must be written in "plain language," meaning that it should be easily read and understood by the CE's patient population.

A valid authorization must include the following information:

- A description of the PHI that the CE plans to use or disclose. The information must be described in a "specific and meaningful fashion."
- The name of the person authorizing the use or disclosure of PHI.
- The name of the person or entity authorized to receive the PHI.
- The purpose of the use or disclosure (the CE can use "at the request of the individual").
- The expiration date of the authorization.
- The authorizing person's signature, and the date the authorization is signed.
- Language that gives the patient the right to revoke the authorization at any time and explains the process for revoking the authorization.
- A statement that the information disclosed may be redisclosed, and may no longer be protected.

- A statement that if the individual does not want to sign the authorization, the CE cannot withhold treatment, payment, enrollment, or eligibility for benefits (unless an exception applies).

The CE must provide a copy of the signed authorization to the individual authorizing the use/disclosure.

Can a CE use or disclose a patient's complete medical record if the patient has signed a valid authorization?

Yes, so long as the authorization signed by the patient includes a specific and meaningful description of the information to be used or disclosed.

That means that the authorization should include language that authorizes the CE to use or disclose an entire medical record or complete patient file. (These terms are preferable to "all PHI" because patients are likely to have a better understanding of medical record than PHI.)

Can a CE use or disclose PHI that was created after an authorization is signed?

That depends. A CE can use or disclose PHI regardless of when it was created so long as that type of PHI is included in the description in the authorization, and the authorization has not expired or been revoked. A new authorization is needed if the CE seeks to use or disclose a type of PHI not included in the original authorization.

Can healthcare providers share PHI for treatment purposes without authorization?

Yes. Healthcare providers such as doctors, nurses, hospitals, and laboratory technicians can use or disclose PHI, such as X-rays, lab reports, and other medical information for treatment purposes without the patient's authorization. This includes sharing the PHI to consult with other providers, (including providers who are not CEs), to treat a different patient, or to refer the patient to another healthcare provider or facility. (See Section 2.5.2.1.2.1.)

2.7.3 Invalid authorizations

An authorization is invalid in these cases:

- The authorization has been revoked by the patient. Patients have the right to revoke their authorization at any time, but must do so in writing, and directly to the CE;
- The authorization has expired; or,
- The information included in the authorization is incomplete, incorrect, or false.

5 Common HIPAA Compliance Myths

Myth #1

"I don't bill Medicare, so I don't need to follow HIPAA Rules"

All covered entities must abide by HIPAA Privacy and Security Rules. Covered entities include healthcare providers, health plans and healthcare clearing houses. Only healthcare providers who do not transmit claims electronically meet an exception.

Myth #2

"As the patient, I own m whole medical record and I want it now."

HIPAA allows individuals the Right to Access and to receive a copy of the Designated Record Set within 30 days. However, the patient does not have ownership of the entire medical record. The provider "owns" the medical record.

Myth #3

"While looking up a patient on the EHR, I accidentally looked up the wrong patient. This is a breach and it needs to be reported."

Not every impermissible use or disclosure is considered a breach. Under HIPAA, there are exceptions to what is a true breach requiring breach notification, such as in this case. Keep in mind that if the impermissible use or disclosure does not meet one of the exceptions, there are strict deadlines to meet under the Breach Notification Protocol to avoid violations and subsequent penalties for untimely reporting.

Myth #4

"Since it was my Business Associate, a billing company that caused the large breach of PHI, I am off the hook."

With a valid written Business Associate Agreement (BAA), this may be true in regard to the financial harm from penalties for a breach by the Business Associate, but this may not prevent significant reputational harm to the covered entity.

Myth #5

"In the waiting room. the nurse should not call out my name [PH when it's time to see the doctor."

This is an example of an Incidental U which is permitted by HIPAA. However, there are many ways tha PHI may be impermissibly disclosed from your facility. An unsuspecting employee can easily b the source of a breach of PHI by simp opening or sending an email.

Chapter 3

The Rights of the Individual Under the HIPAA Privacy Rule

Overview

In this chapter, you will learn about the rights that the HIPAA Privacy Rule gives to individuals with regard to their own protected health information, and how those rights impact covered entities.

Chapter Outline

3.1 The right to access PHI
3.2 The right to request privacy protections
3.3 The right to request amendments of record
3.4 The right to request an accounting of disclosures
3.5 The right to file a complaint

Learning Objectives

After completing this chapter, you should be able to do the following:

- ✓ Explain the rights that individuals have with regard to their health information.
- ✓ Understand how to allow an individual to exercise PHI rights.
- ✓ Understand the concept of no retaliation against an individual wishing to exercise PHI rights.

3.1 The Right to Access PHI

HIPAA addresses the important concept of giving patients access to their own medical information in order to take a more active role in their care. Patients who understand their right to access their protected health information (PHI) and are encouraged to exercise those rights are in a better position to advocate for themselves, communicate with their care providers, manage chronic health conditions more proactively, and to even contribute more meaningfully to research efforts. Patients' periodic review of their own records can also help to identify potential errors in the record.

Patients who review their medical information are better informed, more likely to participate in their own care, and may be able to detect errors in their medical records.

HIPAA provides individuals with the general right to access, inspect, and obtain a copy of their PHI for as long as the information is maintained by a CE or BA, regardless of the date it was created, the format of the PHI, or where the PHI originated. Individuals have the option of requesting a summary or explanation of the PHI. In addition, the right to access also allows individuals to direct a CE to share a copy of their PHI with a designated person or entity.

CEs must include those rights in their Notice of Privacy Practices (NPP). (See Section 2.7.1).

A patient request for access can be made orally or in writing. The Privacy Rule allows CEs to require written requests and to use an entity-supplied form, provided that the form informs individuals of the CE's requirements and provided the CE does not impose unreasonable measures that act as barriers to (or could unreasonably delay) access. HHS lists the following examples as potential barriers:

- If a patient asks to have a copy of their medical records mailed to their home address, the doctor may not require that the person come to the doctor's office to request access and provide proof of identity.
- A doctor may not require an individual to use a web portal for requesting access because not all individuals may have access to the internet.
- A doctor may not require an individual to mail in a request for access because such a requirement could unreasonably delay the CE's receipt of the request and thus, the individual's access to the information.

To avoid barriers or delays, CEs may offer more than one method for patients to request access to their health information.

3.1.1. Verifying the identity of someone who requests access to PHI

In responding to requests for access, the CE is expected to take reasonable steps to verify the individual's identity. The Privacy Rule does not specify a particular form of identification and defers to the CE's professional judgement so long as processes do not create barriers to or unreasonably delay an individual's access.

The form of verification will likely reflect the way that the PHI has been requested or will be shared with the patient. For example, If the patient is completing a form to request access, the form can ask for basic information about the individual that the CE can use to verify the identity of the patient or the patient's personal representative.

3.1.2 Response time to a request for access

A CE must comply with a PHI request within 30 days. If that isn't possible, the entity can obtain a 30-day extension by providing written notice (within the initial 30-day period) to the individual, with the reasons for the delay and date that access will be provided.

According to HHS, CEs are expected to respond well before 30 days, which is considered an outer limit. If a CE is not able to respond in a timely manner, it is encouraged to provide the requested PHI as it becomes available, if the individual is agreeable.

3.1.3 Designated record sets

An individual's right to access applies to PHI contained in a "designated record set." According to the Privacy Rule, a designated record set is a group of records maintained by or for a CE that includes:

- The patient's medical and billing records;
- Enrollment, payment, claims adjudication, and case or management medical records systems kept by or for a health plan; and
- Any other records that are used by or for the CE to make decisions about individuals.

The CE is not required to permit access to PHI that falls outside the scope of the designated record set, because such information is not used to make healthcare decisions. Examples of items that are not considered part of the designated record set include: quality assessment records; patient safety activity records; or, business planning, development, and management records that are used to make business decisions.

Psychotherapy notes recorded by a mental healthcare provider and kept separate from the rest of the patient's medical record are expressly excluded from the right of access (see Section 2.4.4). Also excluded is any information that is compiled by the CE in reasonable anticipation of, or for use in, a civil, criminal, or administrative action or proceeding.

3.1.4 Providing access: format and fees

CEs are expected to provide access to PHI in the form and format requested by the patient, if readily producible. CEs should be able to send PHI by mail or email if requested by an individual; they cannot require the individual to travel to the CE's physical location in order to obtain the requested PHI.

The CE can only charge a reasonable, cost-based fee for providing the PHI. Fees for copies may only include cost of labor, paper or electronic supplies, postage if mailed, and, if requested by the individual, the time to prepare a summary or explanation of the PHI. Costs associated with verification and documentation, searching for/retrieving PHI, maintaining systems, and storage cannot be passed on to the individual.

3.1.5 Denying requests for access

There are a number of reasons why a CE may deny an individual's access to their PHI. A CE must designate a licensed healthcare professional to review patient requests for access to their medical records in order to determine whether it can comply with the individual's request.

If the CE determines that it cannot provide the patient individual with access to the medical record, it must give a reason for denying access. The individual may then challenge that denial and request a review, which must be done by a licensed healthcare professional who did not participate in the original decision. Some of the grounds for denial are reviewable, others are not.

Access can't be denied due to the reason for the request

Patients and authorized individuals are not required to give a reason for requesting access to their medical records.

If the reason for the request is known by the CE because it was given voluntarily by the patient, it cannot be used to deny access to the medical records.

3.1.5.1 Reviewable grounds for denial

If the patient's request for access has been denied for one of the following reasons, the patient can challenge the denial, and it can be reviewed:

- The CE believes that the access requested is reasonably likely to endanger the life or physical safety of the patient. Note that this reason for denial does not apply to a professional's concerns that the access will cause psychological or emotional harm (for example, concerns that the individual will not be able to understand the information or may be upset by it).
- The professional concludes that the access requested is reasonably likely to cause substantial harm to a person referenced in the PHI. (This does not include healthcare providers.)
- The professional concludes that access given to a personal representative of the patient could cause substantial harm to the patient or another person.

3.1.5.2 Unreviewable grounds for denial

If the CE has denied the patient's request for access for one of the following reasons, the patient cannot challenge the denial:

- The request for access is for psychotherapy notes, or for information that has been gathered for use in, or possible use in, a legal action.
- The request for access is made by a prison inmate, and the CE is a correctional institution, or is contracted by the institution to provide healthcare. In this case, if the professional considers that providing access could jeopardize the inmate's health, safety, security, custody, or rehabilitation, or that of other inmates, or the safety of correctional officers, employees, or others, the decision to deny access cannot be reviewed. In such cases, inmates still have the right to view their records, but they cannot obtain hard copies or electronic versions.
- The requested PHI is part of a research study that includes treatment and is still in progress, and the patient agreed to the temporary suspension of access when they agreed to join the study. Once the study is complete, the patient's right to access their PHI is restored.
- The requested PHI is in records protected by the Privacy Act, for example, certain records under the control of a federal agency, which may be maintained by a federal

agency or a contractor to a federal agency. The denial must be consistent with the requirements of the Act.

- The CE obtained the requested PHI from someone other than a healthcare provider (for example, a family member) and promised not to reveal the source, and providing access to the PHI could disclose the source.

3.1.5.3 Communicating denial of access

If a CE denies a patient's request to access their PHI, it must communicate the decision to the patient in writing within 30 days of receiving the request. The CE may take 60 days to communicate the decision so long as it notifies the patient in writing that it needs an extension.

The CE must use plain language to explain why the request has been denied, and it must provide the patient with information about their right to request a review of the denial, provided the reasons for denial are reviewable. Instructions for requesting a review must be included.

If the CE or its BA does not have the PHI in its possession, but knows where it is, it is required to share that information with the patient.

Can an individual access PHI that is held by the BA of a CE?

Yes. If an individual requests access to PHI, it is the CE's responsibility to provide access to the requested PHI that it holds or that a BA holds on its behalf. If both entities hold the same information, it only needs to be provided once to the individual.

The BAA between the CE and BA should clearly state how PHI will be provided to individuals who request access. For example, the BAA may stipulate that the BA will provide the information directly to the individual, or that it will provide the information to the CE to pass along to the individual.

The request must be answered within the 30-day period—or 60 days if an extension applies (see Section 3.1.2)—regardless of which entity is providing the PHI. All access requirements discussed in this section apply to a BA as well as CE.

3.2 The Right to Request Privacy Protections

3.2.1 The right to request restriction of uses and disclosures

Patients can ask CEs to restrict the use or disclosure of their PHI:

- For treatment, payment, or healthcare operations;

- To persons involved in the individual's healthcare or payment for healthcare; or
- To notify family members or others about the individual's general condition, location, or death.

For example, a patient may ask a care provider not to discuss treatment options if the patient's family is in the room.

The CE is not required to comply with a patient's request to restrict access to PHI unless the "pay out of pocket" provision applies (see Section 3.2.1.1). If the CE does agree to restrict access, it must document the restriction in writing and comply with the agreed restrictions, which apply to all future disclosures of the patient's PHI until the agreement is terminated by either the CE or the patient. There is an exception if the patient requires treatment in a medical emergency and the restricted PHI is needed for treatment purposes.

3.2.1.1 Pay-out-of-pocket provision

The pay-out-of-pocket provision gives patients the right to restrict disclosure when they pay for medical services in full. The CE must comply with the request as long as:

- The disclosure is for the purpose of payment or healthcare operations.
- The disclosure is not required by law.
- The PHI only pertains to an item or service for which the individual has paid in full.

3.2.2 The right to request confidential communications

A patient may have concerns about receiving telephone calls, texts, or mail from a CE regarding treatment or payment. HIPAA gives patients the opportunity to express those concerns to the CE. Patients have the right to specify how they would like the CE to communicate with them regarding their medical care and records.

For example, a patient may request that no messages be left on an answering machine, or that all correspondence be sent to a different address than the one listed on the patient's records.

The CE may not question the legitimacy of the patient's concerns. Even if the communication method requested by the patient is not how the CE typically communicates with patients, it must accommodate reasonable requests. The CE is permitted to ask the patient to provide exact details regarding communication and how payment will be handled as a condition of agreeing to comply with the patient's request.

Confidential communication case studies

Hospital implements new telephone messaging policies

A hospital developed and implemented new policies and procedures for contacting family members of patients after an employee did not follow confidential communications requirements or minimum necessary requirements.

The employee called the patient's home phone number and left details of the patient's condition and treatment in a voice mail message on the number, despite the patient's express instructions that she be contacted only on her work phone.

After an OCR investigation, the hospital addressed the issue of leaving only the minimum information necessary on a voicemail message. Employees received training that gave specific instructions about the information that could be left in a message, and were also trained to carefully review patient registration information and to look for specific communication requests made by the patient. The hospital added the new policies and procedures to their standard privacy training for new hires and as part of yearly mandatory refresher training.[7]

Hospital changes patient contact process

A hospital overhauled the way it addressed requests for confidential communications after a patient complained that the hospital had disclosed confidential medical information in a voicemail message on the patient's home telephone, against the patient's express wishes.

To resolve the issue, the hospital:

- Retrained an entire department with regard to the requirements of the Privacy Rule;
- Provided additional specific training to staff members whose job duties included leaving messages for patients; and
- Revised the department's patient privacy policy to clarify patient rights regarding reasonable requests to receive communications of PHI by alternative means or at alternative locations.

3.3 The Right to Request Amendments of Record

If a patient believes that PHI contained in a designated record set is incorrect, the patient can request that the PHI be amended. The CE has 60 days to respond to the request; it can take an additional 30 days if it notifies the patient in writing that it needs more time.

If the CE agrees to amend the PHI, it must capture the change in the patient's record and must make every effort to communicate the change to all individuals and entities that rely on that

[7] https://www.hhs.gov/hipaa/for-professionals/compliance-enforcement/examples/all-cases/index.html#case26

information for treatment purposes. The CE must also let the patient know that the requested amendment has been made.

If the CE denies the patient's request to amend the PHI, it must provide the patient with a written explanation of the denial, and allow the patient to submit a statement of disagreement to be included in the medical record. The explanation must also let the patient know that they can request that the CE provide the amendment request and denial with any subsequent disclosures of the PHI that was the subject of the request. Finally, it must provide instructions for the patient to complain about the decision.

The CE is allowed to draft a rebuttal statement if the patient submits a statement of disagreement. A copy of the rebuttal must be given to the patient.

When a CE amends a medical record and informs another CE or BA of the change, the CE receiving the information must also amend the patient's medical record.

3.4 The Right to Request an Accounting of Disclosures

A patient has the right to request information about disclosures of their PHI made by a CE or BA, with certain exceptions. This is called an accounting of disclosure. Patients can make these requests in writing or orally. If the request is made orally, the CE should document it on a general authorization form or a request for an accounting of disclosures form.

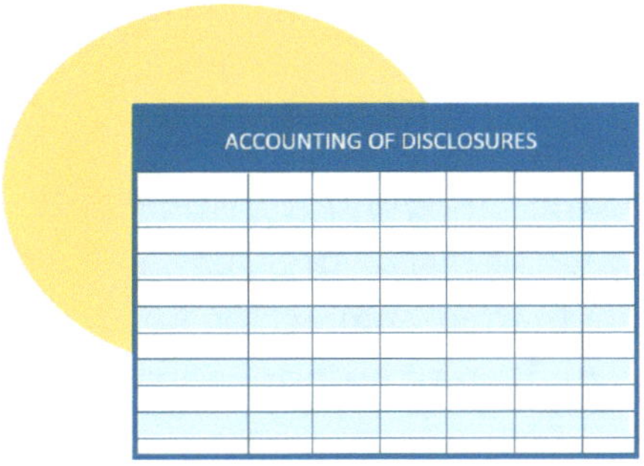

The CE must keep requests for accounting of disclosures with the patient's records, along with a copy of the written accounting provided to the patient. The accounting should also include the name of the person who provided the accounting.

When a patient makes a request for an accounting of disclosure, the request covers a maximum period of six years immediately preceding the accounting request (or a shorter time period if requested by the patient.)

When preparing the accounting of disclosures, the CE does not have to include disclosures made:

- For purposes of treatment, payment, or healthcare operations
- To the patient or personal representative
- To include the patient in a directory
- Pursuant to an authorization

- For national security purposes
- To correctional institutions/law enforcement agencies if related to an inmate or someone in custody
- As part of a limited data set
- Incidental disclosures permitted by the Privacy Rule

The CE must complete the accounting of disclosure within 60 days of the request. If the CE needs more time, it can get a 30-day extension if it provides the individual with a written statement explaining the delay and with the date that the accounting will be provided. The extension request must be made within the first 60 days.

The following information must be provided when responding to such a request:

- The date of disclosure
- The name and address (if known) of the recipient of the PHI
- A brief description of the PHI disclosed
- A brief statement of the purpose of the disclosure

A patient may authorize in writing that the accounting of disclosures be released to another individual or entity. The request must clearly identify all information required to fulfill the request (for example, the name, address, and phone number of the person designated to receive the accounting).

3.4.1 Tracking accounting of disclosures

CEs are required to document the accounting of PHI disclosures provided to patients. The Privacy Rule does not specify how CEs should track accountings of disclosures. CEs can use a tracking process that best fits their operations, ranging from a manual (paper) log kept with the patient's medical records to a computerized tracking system. Patient authorization forms may also serve to track disclosure activity.

Accounting of PHI disclosures made during litigation

If CE discloses a person's PHI for legal proceedings, the CE may be required to include those disclosures in an accounting of disclosures.

The disclosures that must be included in the accounting for disclosures are those disclosures made by a CE that is not a party to the litigation or proceeding, and that are made as required by law; for a proceeding before a health oversight agency; or in response to a subpoena, discovery request, or other lawful process.

CEs do not need to account for disclosures that are made with the authorization of the individual, or if the CE is involved in the litigation, when such disclosures are part of the CE's healthcare operations.

CEs often share PHI for legal purposes with attorneys who are BAs. CEs do not have to account for these disclosures. However, if the attorney discloses PHI that is required to be included in an accounting of disclosures for the reasons listed above, the attorney must provide the CE with the information about the disclosure so that it can be included in the accounting. The attorney can also provide the accounting of disclosure directly to the individual if that option is included in the BAA.

3.5 The Right to File a Complaint

Patients have the right to complain if they believe that a CE or BA has committed a HIPAA Privacy Rule violation, or if they believe the CE or BA has not complied with its own privacy policies and procedures.

The CE must develop and implement a procedure that patients can use to file a complaint. The complaint procedure should include the following:

- A designated staff member who receives and processes complaints.
- Instructions for filing a complaint in the NPP. The instructions should include the name and position of the staff member designated to receive and process complaints, and should inform patients that they have the right to submit complaints directly to HHS. The instructions should also note that the CE cannot retaliate against the patient in any way for filing a complaint.
- A method to receive and document all complaints, such as using a complaint form to capture relevant information from the patient. (A sample HIPAA Privacy Complaint Form is included in Appendix B.)
- Training staff on the proper way to handle a patient HIPAA complaint. (See Section 8.5 on Handling a patient HIPAA complaint.)

A sample HIPAA Privacy Complaint Form can be found in Appendix B of this book.

Chapter 4

Privacy Rule Administrative Requirements

Overview

In this chapter, you will learn about the administrative requirements that covered entities must follow to ensure compliance with the Privacy Rule.

Chapter Outline

Learning Objectives

After completing this chapter, you should be able to do the following:

- ✓ Be familiar with the administrative requirements of the Privacy Rule.
- ✓ Understand how CEs can implement the administrative requirements.

The HIPAA Privacy Rule requires CEs to develop a comprehensive plan to safeguard PHI and avoid prohibited uses and disclosures of the information. Entities that do not develop and implement a plan risk significant fines, costly corrective measures, and damage to their reputations.

The Privacy Rule outlines the following administrative requirements, which are discussed in further detail below:

1. Designate a privacy official
2. Train the workforce on privacy policies and procedures
3. Develop Privacy Rule safeguards
4. Develop a process for filing complaints
5. Establish sanctions for privacy violations
6. Make a mitigation plan
7. No retaliatory acts and no waiver of rights
8. Create policies and procedures for PHI protection
9. Develop a document management policy

4.1 Personnel Designations

CEs must designate an employee to serve as the entity's privacy official. That person is responsible for developing and implementing the entity's privacy policies and procedures. Larger CEs may have a designated compliance officer to manage all HIPAA compliance concerns, while smaller entities often designate an officer with other responsibilities in the company, often someone in an administrative role.

CEs must also designate a contact person or office to receive HIPAA privacy complaints to provide further information about matters covered by the CE's notice of privacy practices (NPP).

As part of the documentation standard (see Section 4.10), CEs must document the name and position of the employee or employees who have been designated as the CE's privacy officials and to receive HIPAA complaints.

4.2 Training

CEs are required to provide all workforce members with the HIPAA privacy training needed to do their respective jobs. Privacy training must be provided to new workforce members within a reasonable time of being hired by the CE. Training should also be given to any workforce member whenever they change jobs or responsibilities, or whenever changes are made to the entity's policies and procedures. In practice, most entities train their workforce annually.

Training must be documented as described in the documentation standard. (See Section 4.10.)

4.3 Safeguards

CEs are required to put administrative, technical, and physical safeguards in place to protect patient PHI.

CEs must use the safeguards to reasonably protect PHI from intentional and unintentional use or disclosure, and to limit incidental uses and disclosures that could result from uses and disclosures that are permitted or required. The following are factors to consider when developing PHI privacy safeguards:

4.3.1 Oral communication

Providers routinely communicate with patients, discuss treatment with colleagues, and exchange information with employees and partners while providing healthcare. Precautions such as these should be taken in order to ensure that PHI is not compromised during typical interactions:

- Staff should not discuss patient information where others can overhear (such as on an elevator or in a waiting room).
- Employees who need to discuss confidential health matters over the phone should make sure they are talking in a private area where they won't be overheard.
- When leaving phone messages for patients, employees should take care to leave the minimum amount of information possible.

Providers should be mindful of their surroundings when discussing confidential medical information with colleagues.

4.3.2 Paper records

All paper records containing patient information should be carefully monitored to ensure that they are not seen or taken by unauthorized parties. Take precautions such as these to protect PHI contained in paper records:

- Take measures to ensure that the information disclosed on sign-in sheets is appropriately limited. For example, do not include the reason for visit or a diagnosis on the sign-in sheet.
- Medical records should not be visible or available to visitors. Label patient files as confidential and turn them face down when not in use.
- Do not leave PHI exposed where others can view it (such as leaving paper charts/imaging studies out on desks or in examining rooms).
- Do not dispose of paper records in regular trash bins. Records must be rendered unreadable, or indecipherable, such as by shredding, and disposed of in secure bins where they cannot be accessed by unauthorized parties.

Improper PHI disclosure by a BA leads to OCR settlement

In February 2018, OCR announced a $100,000 settlement with Filefax, Inc.,[8] a defunct company that once provided medical records storage and disposal services. Based on an anonymous complaint, OCR's investigation uncovered HIPAA Privacy Rule violations due to the company's failure to properly secure patient medical records in its possession.

According to the OCR's investigation, Filefax impermissibly disclosed the PHI of 2,150 individuals in one of two ways:

- Leaving PHI in an unlocked truck in the Filefax parking lot.
- Granting permission to an unauthorized person to remove the PHI from Filefax and leaving the PHI unsecured outside the Filefax facility.

The anonymous complaint alleged that an unauthorized individual was able to retrieve these medical records and attempted to sell them at a shredding and recycling facility. OCR was able to confirm the complaint.

As a BA, Filefax was required to comply with the HIPAA Privacy Rule by implementing appropriate administrative, technical, and physical safeguards to limit incidental disclosures and avoid prohibited uses and disclosures of PHI—including disposal of PHI.

Although Filefax closed its doors in 2017, it was still liable for its violations. As part of the settlement, the court-appointed receiver in charge of liquidating Filefax's assets was not allowed to keep the remaining medical records.

---

[8] https://www.hhs.gov/about/news/2018/02/13/consequences-hipaa-violations-dont-stop-when-business-closes.html

4.3.3 Physical access to PHI

Unauthorized or unsecured access to a CE's place of operation can result in HIPAA violations. CEs should implement practices to ensure that unauthorized individuals do not have access to PHI. This includes the entity's facility and the equipment and spaces used to access, manage and store PHI:

- Implement procedures such as posting signs and locking doors to restrict access so that unauthorized individuals cannot enter the office or healthcare facility.
- Document repairs and modifications to the physical components of facilities that are related to security, such as hardware, walls, doors, and locks.
- Lock desks, cabinets, storage closets etc. where patient records are kept.
- Keep printers, copiers, and fax machines in areas that are not easily accessible to unauthorized persons; do not leave patient records unattended at printers, copiers, or fax machines.

4.4 Complaints to the Covered Entity

CEs are required to develop and implement a process that individuals can use if they have a complaint about the entity's privacy policies and procedures (see Section 3.5). The CE must identify the compliance officer/contact person that is in charge of handling such complaints. Individuals must also be informed that complaints can be submitted to the Secretary of HHS. These procedures must be included in the entity's NPP.

All privacy complaints must be documented, including how the entity addressed the complaint.

4.5 Sanctions

CEs are required to develop and implement sanctions against workforce members who do not comply with the entity's privacy policies and procedures.

This sanctions standard does not apply to a disclosure made by a workforce member who makes a "whistleblower" disclosure to a health oversight agency or public health authority because they believe the CE has broken a law, violated professional standards, or endangers patients, workers, or the public. Likewise, CEs cannot use sanctions to intimidate or retaliate against workforce members who raise privacy concerns.

All sanctions applied against workforce members must be documented.

4.6 Mitigation

CEs must mitigate, to the extent practicable, any harmful effect caused by the use or disclosure of PHI by its workforce or its BAs in violation of its privacy policies and procedures or the Privacy Rule. The entity must include procedures for addressing and correcting privacy violations.

4.7 Refraining from Intimidating or Retaliatory Acts

If employees believe that reporting violations will put their jobs in jeopardy, it is unlikely that they will report violations. CEs may not intimidate, threaten, coerce, discriminate against, or take other retaliatory action against anyone who:

- Files a complaint against the CE regarding a privacy violation
- Provides testimony regarding a privacy complaint
- Makes a whistleblower disclosure

4.8 Waiver of Rights

CEs cannot compel patients to allow their PHI to be used or disclosed. Therefore, CEs may not require individuals to waive their rights under the Privacy Rule as a condition for treatment, payment, enrollment in a health plan, or benefits eligibility.

4.9 Policies and Procedures

CEs are required to implement policies and procedures for complying with the Privacy Rule.

This requirement does not specify the exact policies and procedures that CEs must develop and implement. Rather, it requires that policies and procedures be reasonably designed and be tailored to the size and type of the entity to best address its PHI use and disclosure activities.

If a change to the law requires a CE to make changes to its policies and procedures, the CE must make those changes promptly, and document the changes made. If the changes affect the CE's NPP, the NPP must also be modified to reflect the change.

4.10 Documentation

CEs are required to take the following steps in order to properly document compliance with the Privacy Rule administrative requirements:

- Keep a record of all policies and procedures in written or electronic form
- Keep a record of any written communication related to policies and procedures
- Keep a record of any designation, action or activity related to the Privacy Rule administrative requirements

CEs must also maintain sufficient documentation as a burden of proof, to demonstrate that the appropriate notifications were made in the event of an unauthorized PHI use or disclosure.

CEs are required to retain all documentation required by these Privacy Rule administrative requirements for six years from the date of its creation or the date when it last was in effect, whichever is later. Note that entities should follow their respective state laws on retention periods for medical records. CEs should consider including a plan for tracking document retention and destruction in their policies and procedures as a best practice.

4.11 Group Health Plans

Group health plans are exempted from administrative requirements 4.1 through 4.6 and 4.9 so long as they provide health benefits solely through an insurance contract with a health insurance issuer or an HMO and do not create or receive PHI, apart from summary health information or enrollment information.

These same group health plans must only comply with the documentation requirement (4.10) with respect to changes made to plan documents.

Chapter 5

The HIPAA Security Rule

Overview

In this chapter, you will learn how the need to protect the use, storage, and transfer of electronic protected health information (ePHI) led to the HIPAA Security Rule. You will also learn what constitutes ePHI and the HIPAA rules for safeguarding ePHI.

Chapter Outline

5.1 The Security Rule
5.2 ePHI
5.3 Security Rule Safeguards
5.4 Administrative Safeguards
5.5 Physical Safeguards
5.6 Technical Safeguards
5.7 Organizational Requirements
5.8 Policies and Procedures and Documentation Requirements

Learning Objectives

After completing this chapter, you should be able to do the following:

- ✓ Explain the HIPAA Security Rule.
- ✓ Understand and explain what constitutes ePHI.
- ✓ Understand and list the physical, technical and administrative safeguards for ePHI.
- ✓ Explain how security violations impact individuals and covered entities.

5.1 The Security Rule

Healthcare providers, health plans and their BAs have a strong tradition of safeguarding private health information to keep it from being lost, damaged, or disclosed without permission. However, as covered entities (CEs) began to shift operations to electronic recordkeeping and record-sharing in the 1990s, it became clear that the old systems of locking filing cabinets, marking folders as confidential, and shredding documents would not be enough to safeguard this new form of PHI.

Legislators recognized the need to establish special protections for ePHI, the subset of PHI produced, saved, transmitted, or received in electronic form.

Their efforts led to the creation of the Security Standards for the Protection of Electronic Protected Health Information, also known as the HIPAA Security Rule. The Security Rule was published in 2003 as a component of Title II of HIPAA's Administrative Simplification Rules, and became mandatory in 2005 (2006 for small health plans).

Essentially, the Security Rule complements the Privacy Rule, dealing specifically with ePHI. It establishes a national set of security standards that CEs are required to implement in order to protect ePHI. The standards set forth safeguards to protect ePHI from internal and external threats, such as natural disasters, theft, unauthorized access, hacking, or phishing.

What are some key threats to data security?

- Loss or damage of data due to a system crash, faulty equipment, or power failure
- Loss, corruption or theft of data by computer malware, hackers, or unauthorized users
- Loss or destruction of data due to a natural disaster, act of terrorism, or war
- User error
- Deliberate theft or damage by unscrupulous insiders

At the same time, the Security Rule standards promote the appropriate access, sharing, and use of ePHI by healthcare entities to facilitate interoperability in healthcare operations. In fact, this is one of HIPAA's principal objectives, to support the adoption of industry-wide standards to manage ePHI. Legislators even included financial incentives in the Rule to drive faster adoption of the standards.

In 2009, the Security Rule was reinforced with the passage of The Health Information Technology for Economic and Clinical Health (HITECH) Act, which also expanded the responsibilities of BAs under the Security Rule. In 2013, the Omnibus Final Rule set forth compliance of HITECH regulations and made final modifications to the HIPAA Privacy, Security, and Enforcement Rules.

While the Security Rule establishes a federal floor of standards, state laws that provide more stringent standards will continue to apply over and above the HIPAA security standards.

5.2 ePHI

Under the HIPAA Privacy Rule, PHI refers to all individually identifiable health information (IIHI) held or transmitted by a CE or BA in any form or media, including electronic, paper and oral. A list of the types of PHI can be found in Section 2.4.

The Security Rule protects that subset of PHI that a CE or BA creates, receives, maintains or transmits in electronic form. It does not apply to oral or paper PHI.

Under the Security Rule, the CE is responsible for assuring the confidentiality, availability and integrity of ePHI that it creates, receives, maintains, or transmits, and it must ensure that all employees understand and comply with this mission.

It is important to consider those three words: **Confidentiality** means that ePHI is not available or disclosed to unauthorized persons; **availability** means that it is created and maintained using IT solutions that allow for the safe and expedient storage and transfer of information when needed for permitted uses and disclosures; and **integrity** means that care is taken to ensure that the ePHI is not lost, damaged, or corrupted, so that healthcare providers know that they are working with information that is correct and complete.

Taken together, the terms require CEs to develop a technical set of best practices to ensure that ePHI is properly protected, but can also be efficiently shared among CEs to provide a high level of patient care.

5.3 Overview of Security Rule Safeguards

The Security Rule applies to CEs such as health plans, healthcare clearinghouses, healthcare providers that transmit health information in electronic form, and BAs.

The Security Rule requires CEs and BAs to develop and implement safeguards to protect ePHI. Entities must:

1. Ensure the confidentiality, integrity, and availability of all ePHI they create, receive, maintain or transmit;

2. Identify and protect against reasonably anticipated threats to the security or integrity of the information;
3. Protect against reasonably anticipated, impermissible uses or disclosures; and
4. Ensure compliance by their workforce.

Recognizing that information technology is constantly evolving, and that differently-sized entities require solutions tailored to their operations, the Rule does not specify the technologies that CEs must use. It is designed to be flexible, scalable and technology-neutral, allowing entities to identify the security measures that are the best fit for implementing the standards to protect ePHI. In determining which security measures and technologies are reasonable and appropriate for implementation, the entity should consider the following factors:

- Its size, complexity, and capabilities
- Its technical, hardware, and software infrastructure
- The costs of security measures
- The likelihood and possible impact of potential risks to ePHI

The Security Rule, HITECH and BAs

The 2009 HITECH Act expanded the responsibilities of BAs under the HIPAA Security Rule, and HHS developed regulations to implement and clarify these changes. (See Section 1.2.)

Entities must continually review and modify their security measures to be able to protect ePHI in a changing environment.

The Security Rule requires entities to implement three types of safeguards:

- Administrative safeguards
- Physical safeguards
- Technical safeguards

Safeguards are measures described by the Security Rule to protect ePHI. Each safeguard is made up of multiple standards that address specific situations within the safeguard. Most standards include implementation specifications, some required, some addressable, that provide more detailed guidance on how to implement the safeguard standard.

If an implementation specification is "required," the specification must be implemented. "Addressable" implementation specifications are not optional, but they give entities the flexibility to determine how to best implement safeguards tailored to their operations.

In meeting addressable specifications, entities must do one of the following:

- Implement the addressable specification;
- Implement one or more alternative measures that accomplish the same purpose; or

- Neither implement the addressable specification nor an alternative.

When making this decision, the entity should review factors such as its risk analysis, risk mitigation strategy, security measures currently in place, and the cost of implementation.

If an entity declines to implement an addressable specification, it must carefully document its decision and include the factors considered, including the results of the risk assessment.

5.3.1 Risk analysis and management

Risk analysis and risk management are two implementation specifications of the first administrative safeguard standard. A successful compliance plan hinges on the accurate assessment and management of potential security risks to ePHI, so it is worth considering before continuing on to the specific safeguards.

Security Rule compliance begins with a risk analysis to detect an entity's ePHI risks or vulnerabilities. The entity must use the findings of the risk analysis to develop and implement a risk management plan that is reasonable and appropriate to its size and operations.

A risk analysis process includes (but is not limited to) the following steps:

- Identify potential security threats, including the likelihood of the threat occurring, and the impact
- Determine the security measures necessary to address those risks
- Implement those security measures
- Document the reasons for the implementation
- Periodically review security measures

This last step is important. Risk analysis is an ongoing process. CEs and BAs should periodically reevaluate potential risks to ePHI; review activity to track access to ePHI and detect security incidents; and evaluate the effectiveness of security measures.

The Security Rule safeguards are discussed in further detail in this chapter. Below is the HHS Security Standards Matrix that provides an overview of the types of safeguards and implementation specifications.

HIPAA Security Standards Matrix

Administrative Safeguards

Standards	Sections	Implementation Specifications (R) Required, (A) Addressable	
Security Management Process	§ 164.308(a)(1)	Risk Analysis	R
		Risk Management	R
		Sanction Policy	R
		Information System Activity Review	R
Assigned Security Responsibility	§ 164.308(a)(2)	No separate implementation specifications	
Workforce Security	§ 164.308(a)(3)	Authorization and/or Supervision	A
		Workforce Clearance Procedure	A
		Termination Procedures	A
Information Access Management	§ 164.308(a)(4)	Isolating Healthcare Clearinghouse Functions	R
		Access Authorization	A
		Access Establishment and Modification	A
Security Awareness and Training	§ 164.308(a)(5)	Security Reminders	A
		Protection from Malicious Software	A
		Log-in Monitoring	A
		Password Management	A
Security Incident procedures	§ 164.308(a)(6)	Response and Reporting	R
Contingency Plan	§ 164.308(a)(7)	Data Backup Plan	R
		Disaster Recovery Plan	R
		Emergency Mode Operation Plan	R
		Testing and Revision Procedures	A
		Applications and Data Criticality Analysis	A
Evaluation	§ 164.308(a)(8)	No separate implementation specifications	
BA Contracts and Other Arrangements	§ 164.308(b)(1)	Written Contract or Other Arrangement	R

Physical Safeguards

Standards	Sections	Implementation Specifications (R) Required, (A) Addressable	
Facility Access Controls	§ 164.310(a)(1)	Contingency Operations	A
		Facility Security Plan	A
		Access Control and Validation Procedures	A
		Maintenance Records	A
Workstation Use	§ 164.310(b)	No separate implementation specifications	
Workstation Security	§ 164.310(c)	No separate implementation specifications	
Device and Media Controls	§ 164.310(d)(1)	Disposal	R
		Media Re-use	R
		Accountability	A
		Data Backup and Storage	A

Technical Safeguards

Standards	Sections	Implementation Specifications (R) Required, (A) Addressable	
Access Control	§ 164.312(a)(1)	Unique User Identification	R
		Emergency Access Procedure	R
		Automatic Layoff	A
		Encryption and Decryption	A
Audit Controls	§ 164.312(b)	No separate implementation specifications	
Integrity	§ 164.312(c)(1)	Mechanism to Authenticate ePHI	A
Person or Entity Authentication	§ 164.312(d)	No separate implementation specifications	
Transmission Security	§ 164.312(e)(1)	Integrity Controls	A
		Encryption	A

Organizational Requirements

Standards	Sections	Implementation Specifications (R) Required, (A) Addressable	
Business Associate Contracts or Other Arrangements	§ 164.314(a)(1)	Business Associate Contracts	R
		Other Arrangements	R
Requirements for Group Health Plans	§ 164.314(b)(1)	Implementation Specifications	R

Policies and Procedures and Documentation Requirements

Standards	Sections	Implementation Specifications (R) Required, (A) Addressable	
Policies and Procedures	§ 164.316(a)	No separate implementation specifications	
Documentation	§ 164.316(b)(1)	Time Limit	R
		Availability	R
		Updates	R

Source: *https://www.hhs.gov/sites/default/files/ocr/privacy/hipaa/administrative/securityrule/techsafeguards.pdf?language=es*

5.4 Administrative Safeguards

Administrative safeguards are the administrative actions, policies, and procedures a CE or BA uses to select, develop, implement, and maintain security measures to protect ePHI. Administrative safeguards also include managing the entity's workforce with regard to protecting ePHI and monitoring the ongoing protection of the ePHI.

There are nine administrative safeguard standards established by the Security Rule, detailed below.

5.4.1 Security management process

The first administrative safeguard standard requires CEs and BAs to put policies and procedures in place to prevent, detect, contain, and correct security breaches.

Potential threats to or possible vulnerabilities of ePHI must be identified and analyzed. Entities must continually evaluate the security system to ensure that it is operating according to established policies. Entities should conduct periodic security assessments to determine whether reasonable procedures are in place to protect against threats to the security or integrity of ePHI, as well as procedures to protect against reasonably anticipated uses or disclosures of ePHI by unauthorized personnel.

Entities must update HIPAA-related documents to keep them current with changes to security measures, and should periodically perform technical and non-technical evaluations of Security policies to ensure that HIPAA standards are being met, in particular in the event of environmental or operational changes.

The security management process standard has four implementation specifications:

1. **Risk analysis (Required).** (see also Section 5.3.1). Entities are required to identify potential security risks to and vulnerabilities of all ePHI in their possession. To do this, entities must define how ePHI flows through the organization, track down less obvious sources of ePHI, such as portable devices, identify external sources of ePHI, and assess the human, natural, and environmental threats to information systems that contain ePHI.
2. **Risk management (Required).** Entities must implement security measures to reduce risks and vulnerabilities. Entities can start by assessing the security measures already in place that are used to protect PHI, and then engage executive leadership in risk management and mitigation decisions, to ensure that security processes are being effectively communicated throughout the organization. Other resources that can be deployed to manage risk should also be identified.
3. **Sanction policy (Required).** Entities must devise and apply sanctions against employees who do not comply with security policies and procedures. If an entity already has sanctions in place, those sanctions should be reviewed to ensure that they are sufficient to comply with this specification, or be modified as needed.

   The sanctions policy should include examples of potential violations, and disciplinary action should match the severity of the violation. Employees should sign a statement that they agree to follow the entity's security policies and procedures, and that they understand that they are subject to disciplinary action if they violate them.

4. **Information system activity review (Required).** Entities must develop and implement procedures to review information system activity, including audit logs, access reports, and security incident tracking reports. This review allows entities to determine whether ePHI has been used inappropriately.

   Entities should examine existing information systems to determine whether the audit and review functions are robust, adequately used, and monitored. Logs and reports should be reviewed to ensure that they provide sufficient data on security. The entity must develop a policy to capture in detail how reviews will be conducted.

OCR Security Risk Assessment Tool

The Office of the National Coordinator for Health Information Technology (ONC), in collaboration with the HHS Office for Civil Rights (OCR) and the HHS Office of the General Counsel (OGC), developed a downloadable Security Risk Assessment Tool (SRA Tool) to help guide CEs through the process of conducting a risk assessment as required by the Security Rule. The risk assessment tool can help determine whether a CE is compliant with the Security Rule's administrative, physical, and technical safeguards, and can also identify areas where an organization's PHI could be at risk.

The SRA Tool—which was updated in Fall 2018 to make it easier to use and apply more broadly to health information risks—is a self-contained, operating-system-independent application that can be run on various platforms, including computers and tablets. It takes the user through each HIPAA requirement by asking questions about the organization's activities, and calculating whether the CE needs to take corrective action for a particular item based on the answers provided. Resources are included to help users understand the context of the question, consider the potential impacts if the requirement is not met, and see the actual safeguard language of the Security Rule.

The SRA Tool User Guide can be downloaded at https://www.healthit.gov/sites/default/files/attachmenta-security_risk_assessment_tool_user_guide_v6.pdf

5.4.2 Assigned security responsibility

The second administrative safeguard standard requires entities to designate a security official to be responsible for the development and implementation of the entity's policies and procedures. This requirement is similar to the Privacy Rule requirement for designating a privacy official; an entity may opt to designate the same person as the privacy and security compliance officer.

The security official needs to have good working knowledge of the entity's IT operations in order to be able to create and implement an effective compliance plan to keep ePHI secure. The official is responsible for managing information security policies, procedures, and technical systems.

The designated officer's duties should be clearly identified, documented, and communicated to the officer, and those duties should properly reflect the entity's size and operations.

The assigned security responsibility safeguard standard does not have separate implementation specifications.

5.4.3 Workforce security

The third administrative safeguard standard requires entities to implement policies and procedures that provide workforce members with job-appropriate access to ePHI, and to prevent unauthorized access to ePHI by workforce members who don't need access to ePHI to do their jobs.

The entity should identify workforce members who need access to ePHI to do their jobs, and specify the minimum necessary access needed for each job, as well as the computer systems and programs used to access ePHI. The next step is to implement policies and procedures that ensure only the identified individuals have access to the ePHI on specified computers, systems, and networks.

The workforce security standard has three implementation specifications:

1. **Authorization and/or supervision (Addressable).** Where reasonable and appropriate, entities must implement procedures to authorize and/or supervise individuals who work with ePHI, as well as computer systems that access ePHI.

   To perform this task, entities must designate someone to assign access permissions to ePHI and to develop job descriptions describing the access that different jobs have to ePHI. Entities may already have such rules in place for access to paper-based PHI, and can use those as a starting point for developing ePHI authorization and supervision processes.

2. **Workforce clearance procedure (Addressable).** Where reasonable and appropriate, entities must implement procedures to ensure that workforce access to ePHI is authorized. Entities must provide and restrict access to ePHI in a meaningful way in order to ensure that designated workforce members have access to the information they need to do their jobs.

   Again, entities should start by examining processes already in place for paper PHI, and should check that procedures for determining access to ePHI are used consistently throughout the organization.

3. **Termination procedures (Addressable).** Where reasonable and appropriate, entities must implement procedures for terminating access to ePHI when the relationship with

an employee, contractor, or other individual ends, or when the individual or entity no longer requires access to ePHI.

Termination policies must describe how an individual's access to ePHI will be restricted and the person responsible for terminating access. On the human resources side, there must be procedures in place to inform the person responsible for restricting ePHI access about such terminations in a timely manner.

Former employee costs CE more than $100,000 in HIPAA settlement[9]

A critical access hospital in Colorado agreed to pay a $111,400 settlement with OCR resulting from a complaint that a former Pagosa Springs Medical Center (PSMC) employee had continued to have remote access to the hospital's web-based scheduling calendar after ending their employment.

OCR determined that ePHI of 557 patients was disclosed without authorization to the former Pagosa Springs Medical Center (PSMC) employee.

The CE's failure to deactivate the former employee's access to all systems was a costly lesson in HIPAA compliance.

5.4.4 Information access management

The fourth administrative safeguard standard requires entities to implement policies and procedures for authorizing access to ePHI that are consistent with the Privacy Rule.

This standard requires separating healthcare and clearinghouse services, and limiting access to ePHI to only those workforce members, contractors, and entities that need access. Procedures are needed for granting access that is consistent with a workforce member's need to work with ePHI. Access rights to specific workstations, transactions, programs, or processes should be clearly stated, documented, reviewed, and modified as necessary. In addition, when an individual leaves the organization or changes roles, their access to ePHI should be terminated or modified as appropriate.

As with the workforce security standard, entities must take the Privacy Rule's minimum necessary requirements into account when developing and implementing policies and procedures to comply with this standard, in order to limit unnecessary or inappropriate access to and disclosure of protected health information. (See Section 2.6 on Minimum Necessary requirements.)

[9] https://www.hhs.gov/about/news/2018/12/11/colorado-hospital-failed-to-terminate-former-employees-access-to-electronic-protected-health-information.html

Entities are required to develop policies and procedures regarding the use of workstations, transactions, and software used to access ePHI. Entities should review permissions and modify them as needed.

The information access management standard has three implementation specifications:

1. **Isolating healthcare clearinghouse functions (Required).** Healthcare clearinghouses that are part of a larger organization must implement policies and procedures that separate and protect the clearinghouse's ePHI from unauthorized access by the larger organization. In these cases, the clearinghouse must first determine whether the larger organization also performs healthcare clearinghouse functions, and if so, take care to also protect that ePHI from the larger organization's other operations.

   The clearinghouse should also check whether additional technical safeguards are needed to separate out ePHI in the clearinghouse's information systems, in order to prevent unauthorized access by workforce members from the larger organization.

2. **Access authorization (Addressable).** Where reasonable and appropriate, entities must implement policies and procedures to grant ePHI access through devices and programs such as workstations, transactions, system programs, and processes.

   This safeguard complements the workforce security safeguard. Once an entity has determined *who* should have access to ePHI, it must determine *how* those individuals can access the information. The entity must develop policies and procedures that address how authorization is documented, and how it can be used to provide individuals with access to ePHI. Those policies and procedures must comply with Privacy Rule requirements. Access rules should be job-specific, and technical processes and conventions should be used to ensure appropriate access, such as creating unique user names and implementing an authentication process.

3. **Access establishment and modification (Addressable).** Where reasonable and appropriate, entities are required to implement policies and procedures that establish, document, review, and modify user access to workstations, transactions, programs, and processes based on the policies and procedures developed for access authorization. Policies and procedures should be in place to set up and modify access privileges to ePHI, and those policies and procedures should be documented and updated as needed.

The entity's security officer or another manager should periodically review who has access to ePHI and how access is controlled to ensure that policies and procedures are being properly implemented.

5.4.5 Security awareness and training

The fifth administrative safeguard standard requires entities to implement an ePHI security awareness and training program for all members of its workforce, including management.

Security safeguards can only work if the people charged with implementing and following them understand why the policies and procedures exist, what the potential risks are, and what is expected of them.

Entities must provide comprehensive security training for all new and existing members of its workforce to make sure the workforce is ready and equipped to manage security issues. Workforce members should be retrained whenever external or internal changes happen that could affect ePHI security, such as updates to policies and procedures, updates to system hardware and software, or changes to the Security Rule or state laws.

The security awareness and training standard has four implementation specifications:

1. **Security reminders (Addressable).** Where reasonable and appropriate, entities must periodically update employees regarding changes to security policies and procedures. The entity can use the communication channels that are most effective for their workforce, such as printed or electronic notices, reminders on meeting agendas, and reminders posted around the workplace.

   Entities should also provide workforce members with periodic formal security retraining. All reminder and retraining activities must be documented.

2. **Protection from malicious software (Addressable).** Where reasonable and appropriate, entities must implement procedures for protecting information systems from malicious software and for detecting and reporting malicious software incidents.

   Malicious software refers to viruses, Trojan horses, or worms designed to harm information systems. Bad actors can introduce malicious software (malware) in any number of ways, such as through email attachments or internet downloads, and use it to damage or destroy systems or to steal ePHI. Entities must continually educate workforce members about new threats and about their role in combatting malware attacks.

3. **Login monitoring (Addressable).** Where reasonable and appropriate, entities must implement procedures to monitor attempts to log in to their information systems, and to report any suspected unauthorized login attempts.

   Most systems now incorporate login tracking as a basic capability. Smaller entities or entities with older systems should review their system capabilities to ensure that this specification is properly addressed.

4. **Password management (Addressable).** Where reasonable and appropriate, entities must implement procedures to create, change, and protect passwords. Individuals should be trained on proper password practices, such as using strong passwords, safeguarding passwords, and never sharing passwords with others.

5.4.6 Security incident procedures

The sixth administrative standard requires entities to implement policies and procedures to address security incidents in a timely and effective manner. The Security Rule broadly defines a security incident as unauthorized access, use, disclosure, modification, or destruction of information or interference with system operations in an information system. Incidents include both attempted and successful breaches.

Entities should address all security incidents head on. Waiting to address an issue or attempting to conceal it will only exacerbate an already difficult situation. Detailed procedures should be developed and implemented to address suspected or known security incidents promptly. By taking immediate action, an entity may better mitigate the damage that occurs from a security incident.

The Security Rule requires entities to have a comprehensive plan to manage such incidents, starting with promptly determining whether an incident has occurred and a procedure for notifying the right people. The plan uses the results of the entity's risk analysis to be able to identify and respond to security incidents.

The security incident procedures standard has one implementation specification:

1. **Response and reporting (Required).** Entities must immediately identify and respond to security incidents and take steps to mitigate harm that could result from the incident. Under the Privacy Rule, a BAA must include language that requires the BA to report security incidents to the CE.

   This specification requires entities to document all security incidents, measures taken to address them, and final outcomes. Entities should clearly communicate to workforce members the types of security incidents they may encounter, such as stolen passwords used to access ePHI; corrupted back-ups that result in the loss of ePHI; malicious software attacks; unauthorized access resulting from the use of a terminated employee's credentials; loss or theft of ePHI kept on laptops or mobile devices. Individuals must be trained on how to manage incidents, including reporting protocols, preserving evidence, and assisting with mitigation and documentation.

5.4.7 Contingency plan

The seventh administrative standard requires entities to develop policies and procedures for responding to incidents that can hamper access to ePHI or damage information systems containing ePHI, such as power outages, fire, vandalism, system failure, and natural disasters. An entity's contingency plan must ensure that ePHI is protected at all times and available to authorized users.

The contingency plan standard includes five implementation specifications:

1. **Data backup plan (Required).** Entities must establish and implement procedures to create and maintain exact copies of ePHI that can be retrieved in the event of an emergency. Entities must identify all ePHI to be backed up, and determine the best back-up method, such as tape, disk, CDs, DVDs, or a secure cloud service, and ensure that backed-up ePHI is stored in a safe and secure location. The backup plan must include a back-up schedule designed to minimize information loss in the event of an emergency.
2. **Disaster recovery plan (Required).** Entities must establish procedures to restore data lost during an emergency or other event. The recovery plan must be specific to the entity's operations and allow workforce members to identify the ePHI to be restored. The plan should be kept at multiple locations so that it can be implemented if the entity's location has been affected by an emergency.
3. **Emergency mode operation plan (Required).** Entities must establish procedures that allow them to continue critical business processes that protect ePHI during an emergency.

   The plan should balance the need to access ePHI with the need to protect it during an emergency, and should include alternative security measures, including manual measures, to protect the ePHI. A contact list of all workforce members who should be notified in the event of an emergency, including their roles and responsibilities, should be kept with the plan.

4. **Testing and revision procedures (Addressable).** Where reasonable and appropriate, entities must implement procedures to periodically test and revise contingency plans. The frequency and scope of the testing and revision procedures depend on a variety of factors, such as the complexity of the entity's organization, its size, and the costs of testing and revising plans.

   This specification applies to all plans made under the Contingency Plan Standard: the data backup plan, disaster recovery plan, and emergency mode operations plan. Entities should find ways to test plans, for example by using scenario-based walkthroughs, to ensure that the plans effectively address problems that could arise during an emergency. Testing should be used to ensure that all workforce members with responsibilities during an emergency understand their roles, and that they have participated in testing. Any problems discovered during testing should be addressed by revising plans as needed.

5. **Applications and data criticality analysis (Addressable).** Where reasonable and appropriate, entities must evaluate the criticality of software applications used to store, maintain, and transmit ePHI for providing patient care and conducting business in order to prioritize emergency operations, back-up, and recovery. Entities should draft a prioritized list of specific applications and data to determine the order of restoration and to identify mission-critical applications.

5.4.8 Evaluation

The eighth administrative standard requires entities to perform technical and nontechnical evaluations to respond to environmental or operational changes that could affect the security of ePHI.

Entities can significantly increase their chances of successfully protecting ePHI by testing and evaluating the security safeguards they have put in place. The initial evaluation considers how the safeguards address Security Rule compliance; subsequent evaluations allow entities to examine real-world circumstances to help determine whether their security measures are adequate, and to identify needed changes.

The evaluation standard does not have separate implementation specifications.

5.4.9 Business associate contracts and other arrangements

The ninth administrative standard states that a CE may allow BAs to create, receive, maintain, or transmit ePHI on the its behalf **only** if the CE obtains satisfactory assurances from the BA that it will appropriately safeguard the information. Likewise, a BA may only use a third-party subcontractor to create, receive, maintain, or transmit ePHI on its behalf if it gets similar assurances from the subcontractor.

BAAs between the CE and its BAs must address HIPAA Privacy and Security Rules. (See Section 2.2.2 regarding HIPAA Privacy requirements for BAs.)

The BAA should require BAs to implement appropriate safeguards to prevent unauthorized use or disclosure of ePHI, and require BAs to report any use or disclosure of the information not provided for by its contract.

The CE should request and review BA security compliance plans, and should not enter into a business relationship if a BA does not have one.

The BA contracts and other arrangements standard has one implementation specification:

1. **Written contract or other arrangement (Required).** CEs must document the assurances required by this standard with a written contract such as a BAA.

5.5 Physical Safeguards

Physical safeguards refer to the physical measures, policies, and procedures that an entity uses to protect electronic information systems, facilities, and equipment from natural and environmental hazards and from unauthorized access.

When implementing the physical safeguards, entities must take care to account for all of the ways that ePHI can be physically accessed, both inside the entity's facility and externally, for example, at the homes of employees or other places where they access ePHI.

The Security Rule has four physical safeguard standards.

5.5.1 Facility access controls

The first physical safeguard standard requires entities to implement policies and procedures to limit physical access to information systems and to the interiors and exteriors of the facilities where the systems are kept, while at the same time allowing authorized personnel to access ePHI.

The facilities access controls safeguard has four implementation specifications:

1. **Contingency operations (Addressable).** Where reasonable and appropriate, entities must establish procedures that allow them to execute contingency plans created for the Contingency Plan Standard of the Administrative Safeguards.

   Physical access to facilities varies according to the entity's specific nature and operations. Entities should develop procedures that enable designated workforce members to be able to enter the facility to restore lost data or maintain access to ePHI in an emergency. The plan created for this specification should be included in the entity's contingency plan.

2. **Facility security plan (Addressable).** Where reasonable and appropriate, entities must implement policies and procedures to keep the facility and equipment safe from unauthorized access, tampering, or theft. Physical access controls must ensure that only authorized persons can enter a facility, or specific areas of a facility that contain ePHI.

   Once the entity completes its risk assessment, the results can be used to develop a facility security plan that addresses any issues found in the assessment. Potential controls might include locked doors; use of key cards; surveillance cameras; alarms; restricted area signs; tags or engravings on computers and other property; visitor protocols; and a private security service.

3. **Access control and validation procedures (Addressable).** Where reasonable and appropriate, entities must implement procedures to control and validate access to facilities based on employee roles or functions, including visitor control, and control of access to software programs for testing and revision.

   This specification should align with the facility security plan. It requires procedures to determine which workforce members have access to certain locations within the facility based on their role or function. Possible control measures include requiring proof of identity, key cards, and the use of visitor badges, as well as specific procedures to identify workforce members who are authorized to test and revise software. A list of individuals and their access rights should be included in the facility security plan.

4. **Maintenance records (Addressable).** Where reasonable and appropriate, entities must implement policies and procedures to record repairs and modifications to the physical components of a facility that are related to security, such as changed hardware, repair or removal of walls, doors, or locks, installing new security devices, and routine maintenance.

   Entities can choose the type of maintenance record, such as log book, spreadsheet, or database, that works best for its size and operation. The record should include the following information: changes or repairs made; the date of the change; a description of the work done; who authorized the change; and who made the change or repair.

5.5.2 Workstation use

Workstation security policies and procedures must also be followed by workforce members who work offsite.

The second physical safeguard requires entities to identify the functions that are performed on computer workstations, such as what each workstation is used for, how it is used, and where it is located, in order to protect ePHI that is stored or used on the device.

This standard is designed to help entities avoid inappropriate use of computer workstations that could result in malicious software attacks and confidentiality breaches. Workstations are defined as any computing device, including laptops and desktop computers, electronic media and devices, tablets, mobile phones, servers, and network devices.

The policies and procedures developed for this standard must include policies that apply to workforce members with access to ePHI who work offsite or remotely. Common procedures include training all personnel to log off of their workstations when leaving their work areas, even for a short time, and cooperating with the IT department to make sure that antivirus software is up-to-date on all workstations.

The workstation use standard does not have separate implementation specifications.

5.5.3 Workstation security

The third physical safeguard standard requires entities to implement physical safeguards for all workstations with access to ePHI so that only authorized employees can use the workstations.

Entities must determine who is allowed access to workstations, and create physical safeguards to prevent unauthorized users from accessing or viewing ePHI on workstations. Safeguard measures include:

- Signs
- Physical barriers

- Designating a secure room as the only place where authorized personnel can access ePHI
- Positioning workstation screens away from areas from which they could be viewed
- Privacy screens to prevent others from viewing computer screens
- Cable locks to deter theft
- Port and device locks that physically restrict access to USB ports or CD/DVD drives (unrestricted access to USB ports and removable media devices can facilitate the unauthorized copying of data to removable media)

The physical safeguards used to protect workstations should be documented in the workstation use policies and procedures.

The workstation security standard does not have separate implementation specifications.

5.5.4 Device and media controls

The fourth physical safeguard standard requires entities to implement policies and procedures to control and track the sale, transfer, or disposal of electronic media that is used to store, manage, or share ePHI. Electronic media includes memory devices in computers (hard drives) and any removable digital memory medium, such as magnetic tape or disk, optical disk, or digital memory card.

Suggested methods for removing ePHI from electronic media prior to reuse or disposal

- Clearing the information: The use of software or hardware products to overwrite media with non-sensitive data.
- Purging the information: Degaussing or exposing the media to a strong magnetic field in order to disrupt the recorded magnetic domains.
- Destroying the electronic media: Disintegrating, pulverizing, melting, incinerating, or shredding the media.

CEs may opt to contract with a BA to perform these services.

The device and media controls safeguard has four implementation specifications:

1. **Disposal (Required).** Entities must implement policies and procedures to ensure the proper destruction and disposal of ePHI, including the process for making ePHI unusable and/or inaccessible, and of any hardware or electronic media that it is stored on.

2. **Media re-use (Required).** Entities must implement policies and procedures that describe how ePHI is to be removed from electronic media before that media can be used again, to prevent unauthorized access.
3. **Accountability (Addressable).** Where reasonable and appropriate, entities must track and document movement of ePHI from one location to another, including the person moving the ePHI.

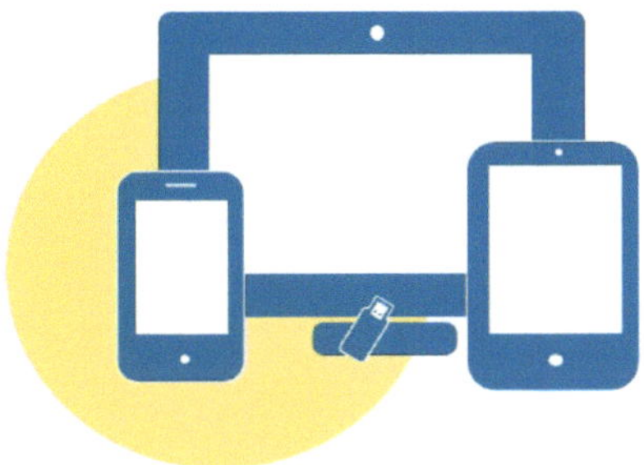

Laptop computers and mobile devices can be challenging to track. The individual responsible for tracking the movement of hardware and electronic media containing ePHI should perform an audit to identify all types of hardware and electronic media used, including laptops, mobile devices, thumb drives, optical disks, etc. The entity may want to assign tracking numbers to these devices and media to facilitate tracking efforts.

4. **Data backup and storage (Addressable).** Where reasonable and appropriate, entities must create a retrievable, exact copy of ePHI, before moving hardware or electronic devices, if the entity considers that a copy is necessary.

   This specification protects the availability of ePHI and is similar to the data backup plan under the Administrative Safeguards (see Section 5.4.7) that requires entities to create and maintain retrievable exact copies of ePHI. For example, an entity might decide to back up a hard drive before moving it, even though the data back-up plan does not include local hard drives. Entities could also provide employees with specific instructions about where ePHI files can be stored, such as designated folders on the network, eliminating the need for local hard drive back-ups.

5.6 Technical Safeguards

Technical safeguards are the technologies used to safeguard ePHI and the policies and procedures that address implementation of those technologies.

Entities use technical safeguards to prevent unauthorized access to ePHI inside and outside of the facility, to maintain the integrity of ePHI, and to track all access.

There are five technical safeguard standards established by the Security Rule.

5.6.1 Access controls

The first technical safeguard standard requires CEs to implement technical policies and procedures to allow access to information systems containing ePHI to only those persons or software programs that have been granted access rights as specified in the Information Access Management standard.

Access is the ability to read, write, modify, or communicate data, to or use a system resource. The access controls standard requires entities to set up a system of rights and permissions to control access to ePHI. The entity must apply the minimum necessary standard to only allow authorized users to access the ePHI necessary to perform their duties, and no more. (See Section 2.6 for Minimum Necessary Standard.)

The access controls safeguard has four implementation specifications:

1. **Unique user identification (Required)**. Entities must assign each workforce member a unique name and/or number to be able to track all ePHI activity by user, and to identify responsible parties in the event of an ePHI security incident.

   Entities can set up their own naming convention, for example, a combination of first and last names. Many entities opt to use randomly assigned user identifiers made up of letters, numbers, and symbols because they are more difficult to hack (although they may also be more difficult for workforce members to remember). Trained IT personnel can help devise strategies that work best for the entity and comply with the requirements of the specification.

2. **Emergency access procedure (Required)**. Entities must establish ways their technology can be used to access ePHI in an emergency. The entity must specify exact practices that designated workforce members can use to get into the system in an emergency.

3. **Automatic logoff (Addressable)**. Where reasonable and appropriate, entities must implement procedures that automatically log a workstation off after a specified time of inactivity. As seen in Section 5.5.2, workforce members should be trained to log off of their workstations when they are finished working. Automatic logoff provides an extra safeguard in case an individual forgets to log off.

4. **Encryption and decryption (Addressable)**. Where reasonable and appropriate, entities must encrypt and decrypt ePHI. Encryption is process of making content unreadable by converting regular text into coded text. Proper use of encryption can prevent unauthorized users from viewing ePHI in a usable form, and can substantially reduce the risk of compromising ePHI.

   Encrypted data involved in a security incident is not considered unsecured ePHI, so breach notification to individuals and HHS is not required (See Chapter 6). This makes a compelling argument for implementing encryption safeguards, even though it is not a required implementation specification.

The case for encryption

In 2012, the individually identifiable health information of more than 13,000 research participants was breached from the Feinstein Institute of Medical Research when an unencrypted laptop left unattended in an employee's car was stolen. The data included names, dates of birth, addresses, social security numbers, diagnoses, laboratory results, medications, and the reason for participation in the study.

A formal OCR investigation found that the Feinstein Institute had an inadequate security management process without proper safeguards to restrict access of unauthorized users, and an absence of policies and procedures addressing the safe removal of ePHI from the facility.

The improper disclosure resulted in a $3.9 million settlement.[10]

Implementing encryption measures may have prevented this HIPAA violation.

5.6.2 Audit controls

The second technical safeguard standard requires entities to implement hardware, software, and/or procedural mechanisms to record and inspect activity in information systems that contain or use ePHI.

Audit controls allow entities to track authorized access and identify potentially unauthorized access to ePHI. These controls are especially valuable when determining whether a security violation occurred. While the standard does not identify data that must be recorded or how often activity should be reviewed, an entity must consider its risk analysis and organizational factors, such as current technical infrastructure, hardware, and software security capabilities, in determining reasonable and appropriate audit controls.

Audit controls can include user activity and access accountability; access and modification of ePHI; log access; and fault logs to detect system errors.

The audit controls standard does not have separate implementation specifications.

5.6.3 Integrity

The third technical safeguard standard requires entities to implement policies and procedures to protect ePHI from being altered or destroyed without authorization. These changes can result in clinical quality problems and patient safety issues.

---

[10] https://www.hhs.gov/sites/default/files/fimr-resolution-agreement-and-corrective-action-plan.pdf

Incidental or intentional changes or destruction of ePHI can be made by workforce members or BAs, and unauthorized changes can also occur without human intervention, for example due to electronic media errors or failures.

Entities must use tools that can confirm that ePHI has not been modified, falsified, or destroyed without authorization.

The integrity standard has one implementation specification:

1. **Mechanism to authenticate ePHI (Addressable).** Where reasonable and appropriate, entities must implement system tools and applications that can verify ePHI has not been altered or destroyed without authorization. The tools and applications should be tailored to address potential risks to the entity's ePHI that were identified in the risk analysis.

5.6.4 Person or entity authentication

The fourth technical safeguard standard requires CEs to implement tools and procedures to verify the identity and authorization of a person or entity who is trying to access ePHI.

Entities need to know and be able to verify that users or other systems are who they say they are, and have authorized access to ePHI. CEs can use unique identifiers to authenticate users, such as passwords, secret words, photo IDs, tokens, badges, or biometric identifiers.

The person or entity authentication standard does not have separate implementation specifications.

5.6.5 Transmission security

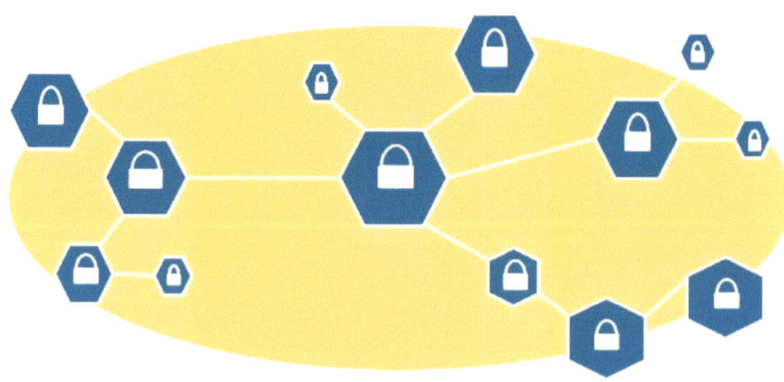

The fifth technical safeguard standard requires CEs to implement technical security measures to protect ePHI from unauthorized access transmitted over an electronic communications network. The entity must review the methods of transmission, such as whether ePHI is sent through email, over the internet, or through some form of private or point-to-point network. Appropriate measures to protect ePHI as it is transmitted must be identified, implemented and documented.

The transmission security standard has two implementation specifications:

1. **Integrity controls (Addressable).** Where reasonable and appropriate, entities must implement security measures to ensure that electronically transmitted ePHI cannot be improperly modified without detection until disposed of.

   The integrity standard discussed in Section 5.6.3 requires entities to protect ePHI that is stored in information systems. This implementation specification focuses on keeping ePHI from being changed or corrupted during transmission. Entities typically rely on network communication protocols to ensure that the data sent is the same as the data received. The entity's security officer should work closely with its IT department and vendor to address integrity controls.

2. **Encryption (Addressable).** Where reasonable and appropriate, entities should encrypt ePHI before it is transmitted. This implementation specification is different from the encryption specification described in the Access Control standard (see Section 5.5.1) because it applies to encryption of ePHI in transit.

   Although the use of encryption is an addressable implementation specification, depending on the entity's business practices, there may be significant risk that ePHI can be accessed by unauthorized entities while the ePHI is being transmitted. If the entity's risk analysis indicates that the entity's ePHI could be vulnerable during transmission, an entity must encrypt those transmissions.

   Entities should discuss encryption needs and methods with their IT team, vendors and BAs. They should periodically reevaluate any encryption measures used to address possible changes in technology and newly emerging threats.

Can CEs legally send ePHI in emails or through the internet?

CEs often wonder whether HIPAA laws permit them to send ePHI in emails, or if they can transmit ePHI over open networks on the internet. While the Security Rule does not prohibit this practice, CEs must implement measures to ensure that transmitted ePHI cannot be accessed by unauthorized users and is protected against damage and loss. CEs must apply the following Security Rule standards when assessing whether these transmission methods can be safely used for ePHI exchange, and to develop and implement procedures: Access control (see Section 5.6.1); integrity (see Section 5.6.3); and transmission security (see Section 5.6.5).

Patients can initiate communications with a healthcare provider using email. If a patient emails a provider, the provider can assume (unless the patient has explicitly stated otherwise) that the patient agrees to communicate via email. However, if the provider believes the patient may not be aware of the possible risks of using unencrypted email, or has concerns about potential liability, the provider can alert the patient of those risks, and let the patient decide whether to continue to communicate with email.

5.7 Organizational, Policies and Documentation Requirements

In addition to administrative, physical, and technical safeguards, the Security Rule includes four standards that define the organizational, policies and procedures, and documentation requirements of the Rule.

5.7.1 Business associate contracts or other arrangements

The first organizational requirement standard requires CEs to have contracts or other arrangements with BAs that have access to the CE's ePHI. The standard specifies what must be included in a BAA.

This standard has one implementation specification for BA contracts. The CE and BA must enter into a BAA specifying that the BA will ensure that any of its subcontractors that handle a CE's ePHI on its behalf will enter into a contract with the BA that also requires compliance with HIPAA. The BAA must also require the BA to report any security incidents, including breaches of unsecured PHI, that it becomes aware of to the CE. Lastly, a BA and its subcontractor must enter into a contract similar to the BAA.

5.7.1.1 The business associate agreement

Once a CE determines that an entity or individual with which it has a business relationship meets the HIPAA definition of a BA, the CE is responsible for ensuring that the third party complies with HIPAA privacy regulations and appropriately safeguards PHI that it receives or creates on behalf of the CE. According to HIPAA rules, those assurances must be in captured in a written agreement between the CE and BA.

A sample **Business Associate Agreement** can be found in Appendix B of this book.

The BAA specifies each party's responsibilities with regard to PHI. The BAA must specify the permitted and required PHI uses for the BA, state explicitly that the BA will not use or disclose the PHI for any purpose other than those stated in the agreement, and require the BA to implement safeguards to prevent any PHI use or disclosure not specified by the contract.

A BAA must contain specific language in order to comply with HIPAA. The BAA must:

- Establish the permitted and required uses and disclosures of PHI by the BA;
- State that the BA will not use or disclose PHI for any reasons other than those permitted or required by the BAA or required by law;
- Require the BA to implement safeguards to prevent unauthorized use or disclosure of the PHI, including implementing requirements of the HIPAA Security Rule with regard to ePHI;

- Require the BA to report any use or disclosure of the information not provided for by its agreement to the CE, including breaches of unsecured PHI. (See Section 8.8 for more detail on how to address breaches in the BAA);
- Require the BA to disclose PHI on behalf of the CE with respect to individuals' requests for copies of their PHI, and to make PHI available for amendments and accountings;
- To the extent that the BA must carry out a CE's obligation under the Privacy Rule, the BAA must require the BA to comply with the requirements applicable to the obligation;
- Require the BA to make available its internal practices, books, and records relating to the use and disclosure of PHI to HHS for HHS investigations;
- If feasible, the BAA must require the BA to return or destroy all PHI when the BAA is terminated;
- Require the BA to ensure that any subcontractors it uses that will have access to PHI agree to the same restrictions and conditions that apply to the BA with respect to such PHI; and
- Authorize the CE to terminate the BAA if the BA violates a term of the agreement.

Tips for negotiating BAAs

- Consider unique privacy and security issues presented by the BA and CE relationship, such as whether PHI will be stored in the cloud or if PHI will be aggregated or used for data analytics.
- Determine the level of risk presented by the CE and BA relationship and tailor the BAA accordingly.
- Maintain an appropriate level of cyber liability insurance.
- Obtain legal counsel to prepare a BAA that fits your contracting needs.

5.7.2 Requirements for group health plans

The second organizational requirement standard requires CEs that are group health plans to require the plan sponsor to safeguard ePHI that it creates, receives, maintains, or transmits on behalf of the plan.

The requirements for the group health plans standard has one required implementation specification that sets out the requirements for the plan documents of the group health plan. These plan documents must include provisions that require the plan sponsor to:

1. Implement administrative, technical, and physical safeguards for ePHI that the sponsor creates, receives, maintains, or transmits on behalf of the group plan;
2. Implement appropriate security controls to ensure adequate separation between plan sponsor employees who use and disclose ePHI;
3. Ensure that other parties that receive ePHI from the plan sponsor agree to protect ePHI by implementing appropriate security measures; and
4. Report all security incidents it becomes aware of to the group health plan.

5.7.2.1 Policies and procedures

The Security Rule requires entities to document and create written policies and procedures for nearly every administrative, physical, and technical safeguard requirement. While this standard requires entities to implement reasonable and appropriate policies and procedures, it does not define the exact content or format. The Rule's flexibility and scalability permit entities to determine how to address these tasks and tailor them to their own size and business type in order to reflect the entity's mission and culture. This standard is further supported by the Documentation standard.

Generally, the term policy is understood to mean the entity's approach to addressing the Security Rule safeguards, for example objectives, decision-making responsibilities, and the consequences of violations. Procedure refers to the detailed instructions of how that approach is implemented.

The policies and procedures standard does not have separate implementation specifications.

5.7.2.2 Documentation

This standard requires entities to document the policies and procedures that they implement to comply with the Security Rule. Any action, activity, or assessment taken by the entity in order to comply with the Security Rule must also be documented. The entity can keep paper or electronic records to document policies, procedures, and other related activities.

The documentation standard has three required implementation specifications:

1. **Time Limit (Required).** Entities must retain the documentation of all policies and procedures for a minimum of six years from the date of their creation or the date when they were last in effect, whichever is later. Entities may opt to keep their documentation for longer periods of time based on state law or for other business reasons.

2. **Availability (Required).** Entities must make documentation available to those persons responsible for implementing procedures, such as making documentation available in printed or electronic manuals.
3. **Updates (Required).** Entities must periodically review documentation and make appropriate updates in response to environmental or operational changes affecting the security of ePHI.

Chapter 6

The HIPAA Breach Notification Rule

Overview

In this chapter, you will learn about the notification requirements that CEs and BAs must follow in the event of a PHI breach.

Chapter Outline

6.1 The HIPAA Breach Notification Rule
6.2 Breach notification requirements
6.3 Administrative requirements and burden of proof

Learning Objectives

After completing this chapter, you should be able to do the following:

- ✓ Understand what constitutes a breach of unsecured PHI, the exceptions to a breach, and determining whether a breach triggers notification requirements.
- ✓ Be able to state the requirements for breaches of different sizes.
- ✓ Know the administrative requirements for the Breach Notification Rule.

6.1 The HIPAA Breach Notification Rule

The HIPAA Privacy and Security Rules require CEs and their BAs to make every reasonable effort to protect PHI in all its forms from unauthorized use or disclosure. Chapter 4 addresses the administrative requirements that entities must follow to ensure compliance with the Privacy Rule, and Chapter 5 addresses the safeguards that entities must implement under the Security Rule to protect the integrity, privacy and availability of ePHI.

Despite best efforts, however, an entity may suspect or discover that it has suffered a PHI breach. When that happens, entities must have policies and procedures in place to quickly and effectively report PHI breaches.

The HIPAA Breach Notification Rule requires CEs to notify affected individuals, HHS, and, in some cases, the media of a breach of ***unsecured*** PHI, and requires BAs to notify the CE about breaches.

Under this Rule, a breach is broadly defined as an impermissible use or disclosure of unsecured PHI that compromises the affected individuals' security or privacy.

Unsecured PHI is PHI that has not been made unusable, unreadable, or indecipherable through encryption or destruction.

- Encryption: An algorithmic process used to convert data into a form that cannot be understood without the use of a similar process or key to decrypt the data. The confidential process or key should be stored on a separate, secured device or at a separate location from the encrypted/decrypted data in order to avoid a breach. Encrypted data that has been accessed by an unauthorized person or system is considered secure if the unauthorized party has not gained access to the decryption process or key. This is why encryption is critical even though it is not a required specification under the HIPAA Security Rule. (See Section 5.6.5.)
- Destruction: Shredding or otherwise destroying paper, film, or other hard copy media in such a way that the PHI cannot be read or reconstructed. Destruction of ePHI stored on electronic media requires clearing, purging, or destroying the data.

Examples of unsecured PHI include stolen paper medical files, or a lost or stolen laptop containing unencrypted patient information.

6.1.1 Exceptions to a breach

Not every incident of unauthorized PHI use or disclosure constitutes a HIPAA breach that would trigger notification protocols. There are three exceptions to the definition of a breach:

1. A workforce member or person acting under the authority of a CE or BA unintentionally accesses or acquires PHI in good faith and within the scope of authority. The PHI is not further used or disclosed in a manner not permitted by the Privacy Rule. For example: An accountant working for a BA inadvertently accesses a patient's medical history when reviewing financial documents.

Unintentional access to PHI by an individual who works with an entity is not considered a breach if the first exception is fully met.

2. A workforce member authorized to access PHI at a CE or BA inadvertently discloses PHI to another person authorized to access PHI at the CE or BA, or organized healthcare arrangement in which the CE participates. The PHI is not further used or disclosed in a manner not permitted by the Privacy Rule. For example: A nurse overhears a doctor discussing a case that he is not involved with, and does not share the information with anyone else.
3. The CE or BA has a good-faith belief that the unauthorized party that received the PHI would not have been able to retain the data. For example, an entity sends an explanation of benefits (EOB) to the wrong person, and the EOBs is returned to the entity unopened by the post office. Even though the confidential information was sent to the wrong person, it is reasonable to assume that the unauthorized person did not actually look at the information, because it was returned unopened.

6.1.2 Assessing whether PHI has been compromised

Unless one of the exceptions to a breach listed in 6.1.1 applies, an impermissible use or disclosure of unsecured PHI is presumed to be a breach. The CE or BA must move on to the next step: conducting a risk assessment to determine the probability that PHI has been compromised.

At a minimum, the risk assessment must consider the following four factors:

1. The nature and extent of the PHI involved, including the types of identifiers and the likelihood of re-identification;
2. The unauthorized person who used the PHI or to whom the disclosure was made;

3. Whether the PHI was actually acquired or viewed; and
4. The extent to which the risk to the PHI has been mitigated.

If the risk assessment indicates that there is more than a low probability that the PHI has been compromised, the breach must be reported following the procedure set forth in the Breach Notification Rule. If the breach occurs at a BA, the BA must notify the CE according to the terms and conditions in the BAA.

6.2 Breach Notification Requirements

6.2.1 Individual notice

If a CE discovers a breach of unsecured PHI, and a risk assessment indicates that there is more than a low probability that the PHI is compromised, the Breach Notification Rule requires the CE to notify affected individuals.

The Rule requires CEs to provide written notice by first-class mail. CEs may provide notice via email if the individual(s) affected by the breach have previously agreed to this. If the CE does not have correct contact information for ten or more affected individuals, it must use a different way to reach individuals, either posting the notice on the home page of its website for at least 90 days, or providing the notice in major newspapers or broadcast media in the affected individuals' area(s).

The CE must include a toll-free telephone number that individuals can call to receive information about the breach (for example, whether their PHI is involved in the breach). The phone number must remain active for at least 90 days.

If the CE is missing contact information for fewer than ten individuals, it can provide notice by written notice, telephone, or other means. Notice in public media is not required.

CEs must provide individual notifications as quickly as reasonably possible, and no later than 60 days after the discovery of a breach. The notifications should include the following:

- A description of the breach.
- A description of the types of information that were breached.

- The steps affected individuals should take to protect themselves from potential harm.
- A description of how the CE is managing the breach: investigating the breach, mitigating the harm, and preventing future breaches.
- Contact information for the CE (or BA, as applicable).

If a BA suffers a breach, the CE is responsible for making sure that individuals are notified, although it is permitted to delegate notification efforts to the BA. The CE and BA should work together to determine which entity is best suited to notify affected individuals, which will depend on several factors, such as the BA's services, and which entity has the relationship with the affected individuals.

6.2.2 Media notice

If a breach affects more than 500 individuals living in the same state or jurisdiction, the CE must carry out the notification efforts for individuals explained in 6.2.1. I addition, the CE is required to issue a press release notifying the major print and broadcast media outlets in the area of the breach.

As with individual notice, the CE must alert the media as quickly as reasonably possible, and no later than 60 days after the discovery of a breach. The press release must include the same information required for individual notice.

6.2.3 Notice to the HHS

CEs must also notify the HHS Secretary of any unsecured PHI breaches. To notify HHS, the CE goes onto the HHS website and completes and submits a breach report form online.

If a breach affects 500 or more individuals, the CE must notify HHS as quickly as reasonably possible, and no later than 60 days after the discovery of a breach. If a breach affects fewer than 500 individuals, the CE can notify HHS in an annual report. A breach of this size must be reported no later than 60 days after the end of the calendar year in which it is discovered.

6.2.4 Notification by a BA

As noted above, a BA must notify the CE in the event of an unsecured PHI breach. The BA must alert the CE as quickly as reasonably possible, and no later than 60 days after the breach is discovered.

To the best of its ability, the BA should provide the CE with a list of affected individuals and with information the CE needs to comply with the notification requirements of the Rule.

A costly lesson in untimely reporting of a HIPAA breach

In January 2014, Presence St. Joseph Medical Center (a hospital of Presence Health Network, a large healthcare system serving Illinois) notified HHS that it had discovered a breach more than three months earlier involving 836 individuals. The untimely reporting cost the healthcare system a $475,000 settlement with HHS, and strict compliance with a two-year corrective action plan that impacted all 150 locations of Presence Health Network.[11]

Presence discovered in October 2013 that paper operating room schedules were missing from its facility. The schedules contained the PHI of 836 individuals, specifically individuals' names, dates of birth, medical record numbers, dates of procedures, types of procedures, surgeon names, and types of anesthesia administered.

Under the HIPAA Breach Notification Rule, because the breach affected more than 500 individuals, Presence was required to notify the affected individuals, HHS, and major media outlets no later than 60 days after the breach. Nevertheless, it took Presence 101 days to report the breach to the government, citing miscommunication issues between staff for the delay.

HHS investigated the breach and found that Presence had not only taken too long to report the breach to HHS, but it had also not met the deadline for notifying affected individuals and media outlets.

HHS reviewed other breach events that occurred at Presence in 2015 and 2016 and uncovered a pattern of delayed reporting. Because these breaches had affected less than 500 individuals, Presence was required to notify affected individuals no later than 60 days after the breach, and notify HHS no later than 60 days after the end of the calendar year. However, in each of the instances, Presence failed to follow timely reporting requirements.

6.3 Administrative Requirements and Burden of Proof

Entities are required to provide proof to HHS that they have complied with the reporting requirements of the Breach Notification Rule. Careful documentation that demonstrates the entity's notification efforts should be kept and saved.

If an entity concludes that an unauthorized use or disclosure was not a breach (see Section 6.1.1), or that PHI was not compromised (see Section 6.1.2), the entity must be able to support that conclusion. Supporting documentation includes a detailed explanation of how the incident qualifies as an exception to a breach, or the risk assessment demonstrating that there is a low probability that PHI was compromised.

Entities must develop and implement written policies and procedures regarding breach notification, and must train workforce members so that they have a clear understanding of their role and responsibilities with respect to breach notification protocols. Policies and procedures should include sanctions against workforce members who do not comply with notification responsibilities.

[11] https://www.hhs.gov/sites/default/files/presence-ra-cap.pdf

Chapter 7

The HIPAA Enforcement Rule

Overview

In this chapter, you will learn how the Security Rule was reinforced with the passage of the Health Information Technology for Economic and Clinical Health Act (HITECH), and you will learn about the final modifications to HIPAA made by the Omnibus Final Rule. You will also learn about the HIPAA Enforcement Rule's provisions for proper compliance and investigations, and for imposing monetary penalties for HIPAA violations.

Chapter Outline

7.1 The HIPAA Enforcement Rule
7.2 HIPAA enforcement agencies
7.3 HIPAA enforcement and penalties
7.4 HIPAA enforcement efforts
7.5 HIPAA enforcement case summaries

Learning Objectives

After completing this chapter, you should be able to do the following:

- ✓ Understand the provisions of the HIPAA Enforcement Rule.
- ✓ Learn more about the agencies charged with enforcing HIPAA.
- ✓ Be familiar with the monetary, civil, and individual liabilities.
- ✓ Be aware of types of HIPAA enforcement and penalties.

7.1 The HIPAA Enforcement Rule

The HIPAA Enforcement Rule contains provisions for HIPAA compliance and investigations, provisions for imposing monetary penalties for HIPAA Privacy and Security violations, and provisions for hearings procedures.

With the passage of the HITECH Act in 2009, CEs and BAs became equally liable for violations of administrative simplification, and a penalty of up to $1.5 million per violation per calendar year was established. This penalty applies even if the CE did not know about a violation. The Omnibus Final Rule finalized the HITECH changes and mandated compliance in 2013.

HIPAA violations can result in potentially harsh consequences, such as steep fines and even criminal charges.

The Omnibus Final Rule also instituted changes specific to the HIPAA Enforcement Rule. These changes included addressing enforcement of noncompliance with the HIPAA Rules due to willful neglect, i.e. conscious intentional failure or reckless indifference; and increasing and creating a tiered civil money penalty structure.

7.2 HIPAA Enforcement Agencies

A number of federal agencies are involved in enforcing HIPAA regulations:

The Office for Civil Rights (OCR). The OCR is charged with protecting health information privacy rights. The agency investigates health information privacy and patient safety confidentiality complaints. It also engages in education activities for health and social service workers and community members about health information privacy and patient safety confidentiality laws.

Center for Medicare and Medicaid Services (CMS). CMS works with healthcare providers, health plans and clearinghouses to help them with HIPAA compliance through education and complaint-driven enforcement. CMS has the authority to investigate HIPAA complaints and perform audit compliance for transactions, code sets, unique identifiers and operating rules.

Department of Justice (DOJ). The OCR works in conjunction with the (DOJ) to investigate and impose consequences for criminal violations of HIPAA.

Pursuant to the HITECH Act, enforcement authority is also granted to States Attorney General to bring civil actions on behalf of state residents for violations of the HIPAA Privacy and Security Rules.

7.3 HIPAA Enforcement and Penalties

OCR HIPAA enforcement activity consists of conducting compliance reviews of CEs and BAs, as well as investigating HIPAA complaints filed with the agency.

When a compliance review, notification of a breach, or HIPAA complaint reveals that a CE is in noncompliance, OCR will typically first try to work with the entity to resolve the issue. Possible outcomes include voluntary compliance by the CE, corrective action, or a resolution agreement.

HIPAA violations can also result in civil and criminal penalties. If a review or complaint reveals activity that could be a violation of the criminal provisions of HIPAA (violations that were committed "knowingly"), OCR may refer the complaint to the DOJ for investigation.

7.3.1 Civil monetary penalties

For non-criminal violations, if the CE does not resolve the matter to the OCR's satisfaction, the agency may impose civil monetary penalties.

The Enforcement Rule uses a four-tiered civil penalty structure. The HHS Secretary has discretion in determining the amount of the penalty, based on the type and extent of the violation and the harm resulting from the violation. Penalties for willful neglect are mandatory.

The Secretary takes any corrective action taken by the CE into account, and cannot impose civil penalties (except in cases of willful neglect) if the violation is corrected within 30 days. HHS has the authority to extend this time period.

7.3.1.1 Factors that determine civil monetary penalties

The following factors can impact the type and amount of a penalty:

- The type and extent of the HIPAA violation, including such factors as the number of individuals affected by the breach and the time period over which the breach occurred.

- The type and extent of harm caused by the breach, including:
    - Physical harm.
    - Financial harm.
    - Harm to an individual's reputation.
    - Whether the violation interfered with an individual's ability to access healthcare.
- The entity's compliance history, including:
    - Whether the violation is the same or similar to previous violations.
    - The entity's efforts to correct previous noncompliance issues.
    - The entity's response to technical assistance from HHS.
    - The entity's response to previous complaints.
- The entity's financial situation, including:
    - Whether financial difficulties hampered the entity's compliance efforts.
    - Whether a monetary penalty could put the entity's ability to continue to provide healthcare in jeopardy.
    - The size of the entity.
- Other factors that enforcement agencies deem relevant.

7.3.2 Tiers of civil monetary penalties

The OCR assesses four tiers of civil penalties for HIPAA violations:

HIPAA Violation	Minimum Penalty	Annual Limit
Unknowing	$100 per violation	$25,000
Reasonable Cause	$1,000 per violation	$100,000
Willful neglect but violation is corrected within the required 30-day time period	$10,000 per violation	$250,000
Willful neglect and is not corrected within required time period	$50,000 per violation	$1,500,000

This penalty tier structure was released in a Notification of Enforcement by the Department of Health and Human Services (HHS) on April 30, 2019, and will be adjusted for inflation. The Federal Civil Penalties Inflation Adjustment Act Improvements Act of 2015 directs agencies such as the HHS to adjust civil monetary penalties (CMPs) for inflation based on a prescribed formula. New CMP amounts are published annually in the Federal Register.

7.3.3 Reduced or no civil penalties

HHS may waive or reduce civil penalties for HIPAA violations if the CE or BA had no knowledge of the violation, or it would not have been known even with reasonable due diligence.

If HHS finds that there was "reasonable cause" for the violation, it was remedied in 30 days, and there was no finding of willful neglect, it may also elect to waive or reduce the penalties.

If a criminal violation has been committed, HHS will typically not pursue civil violations, because criminal penalties will likely be imposed.

7.3.4 Criminal penalties

Criminal violations of HIPAA are handled by the DOJ. Like the OCR, the DOJ imposes criminal penalties of varying severity depending upon the nature and the extent of the violation. Criminal penalties include monetary penalties and imprisonment.

HIPAA CEs that knowingly obtain or disclose PHI can face a fine of up to $50,000, as well as imprisonment up to 1 year. That fine will increase to $100,000 and five years in prison if the DOJ finds that the offense was committed under false pretenses.

If an offense is committed with the intent to sell, transfer, or use PHI for commercial advantage, personal gain, or malicious harm, a fine of up to $250,000 could be imposed, along with and up to 10 years of imprisonment.

HIPAA Violation	Monetary Penalty	Prison Sentence
Knowingly obtain or disclose PHI	$50,000	Up to 1 year in prison
Using, obtaining or disclosing PHI under false pretenses	$100,000	Up to 5 years in prison
Intent to use PHI for advantage, gain, or harm	$250,000	Up to 10 years in prison

Individuals involved in HIPAA violations can be held personally liable for incidents occurring at the entities where they work.

Individual liability includes employee liability for the employee's own conduct; liability of privacy officers; entity liability for the acts of employees; and concurrent liability of employees and the entity.

Individual liability for corporate misconduct is emphasized in the "Yates Memo," a memorandum issued on September 9, 2015 by then-DOJ Deputy Attorney General Sally Q. Yates. In the memo, Yates outlined how federal investigations should be conducted in cases involving corporate fraud or misconduct. The memo was not issued specifically for the healthcare industry, but the item regarding individual responsibility applies to CEs and BAs in a HIPAA violation case. On November 29, 2018, the DOJ announced changes to the Yates Memo that provided more flexibility to DOJ attorneys in resolving these types of matters.

7.4 HIPAA Enforcement Efforts

OCR Enforcement Activity since 2003 ***(numbers current to August 2017)***	
Complaints received	184,614
Compliance reviews initiated	902
Cases resolved	177,194
Cases resolved by requiring changes in privacy practices and corrective actions by, or providing technical assistance to CEs and their BAs	26,071
Cases where civil money penalties were imposed	55
Total amount of penalties imposed	$78,829,182
Cases where investigations found no violation occurred	11,494
Cases where OCR has intervened early to provide technical assistance	28,450
Cases the OCR did not pursue (due to such reasons as non-CE, activity not a HIPAA violation, withdrawn complaint)	111,179
Most-investigated compliance issues investigated, in order of frequency	• Impermissible uses and disclosures of PHI • Lack of safeguards of PHI • Lack of patient access to their PHI • Lack of administrative safeguards of ePHI • Use or disclosure of more than the minimum necessary PHI
Most common types of CEs required to take corrective action to achieve voluntary compliance, in order of frequency	• General Hospitals • Private Practices and Physicians • Outpatient Facilities • Pharmacies • Health Plans (group health plans and health insurance issuers)

Source: *https://www.hhs.gov/hipaa/for-professionals/compliance-enforcement/data/enforcement-highlights/2018-june/index.html*

OCR tracks enforcement activity and cumulative enforcement results starting from when the HIPAA Privacy Rule was implemented in 2003 up to the present. Data includes the number of cases in which OCR obtained corrective action, did not find violations, referred the case to DOJ, or otherwise resolved.

The DOJ does not make data compilations available on criminal HIPAA convictions, although the agency does release notices regarding HIPAA indictments and convictions and posts them on the DOJ website.

7.5 HIPAA Enforcement Case Summaries

The case summaries below are not a comprehensive or representative list of enforcement actions. However, they serve to illustrate the different types of HIPAA violations that CEs have experienced and the penalties imposed.

Ex-employee at UCLA Healthcare pleads guilty to HIPAA violations[12]

A UCLA researcher was sentenced to four months of prison and fined $2,000 in April 2010 after he pled guilty to accessing and reading the health records of celebrities and co-workers. The researcher, a UCLA Health System employee, was the first person ever to receive a prison sentence for a misdemeanor HIPAA violation.

The employee accessed the confidential records over a three-week period in 2003 shortly after being fired. Although he did not profit from the use or sale of the information, he was found to have violated HIPAA rules because he did not have a reason or proper authorization to access the records. In addition to the sanctions against the individual, UCLA agreed to pay a civil fine of $865,000 stemming from complaints that its employees had viewed celebrities' medical records without authorization. A federal investigation found that UCLA employees had accessed confidential records "repeatedly and without a permissible reason" hundreds of times between 2005 and 2009. The investigation also found that the entity took no steps to remedy the problem and discipline or retrain its staff.

Dermatology practice pays $150,000 fine after unencrypted flash drive stolen[13]

A Massachusetts dermatology practice agreed to pay a $150,000 fine in 2013 for HIPAA violations after the practice reported a breach resulting from a lost, unencrypted flash drive that contained the ePHI of 2,200 individuals. The investigation found that the 12-physician group did not conduct an accurate and thorough risk analysis; did not fully comply with the administrative requirements of the Breach Notification Rule, and failed to safeguard ePHI by storing it on an unencrypted drive that was stolen from a workforce member's car.

---

[12] *United States v. Zhou*, 678 F.3d 1110 (9th Cir. 2012).

[13] https://www.hhs.gov/sites/default/files/ocr/privacy/hipaa/enforcement/examples/apderm-resolution-agreement.pdf

Physician convicted of HIPAA violation for sharing PHI with pharmaceutical rep[14]

A Massachusetts gynecologist was convicted by a jury in 2018 for giving a pharmaceutical sales representative access to patient files in return for kickbacks, and for providing false information during a federal investigation. The doctor was sentenced to one year of probation.

$100,000 settlement for failure to implement HIPAA requirements[15]

An Arizona-based cardiology group agreed to pay a $100,000 settlement in 2012 for failing to comply with even the most basic HIPAA privacy and security rules. The OCR investigated the group after learning that it was posting clinical and surgical appointments for patients on a publicly accessible online calendar. Privacy and Security rule violations included failure to implement adequate policies and procedures to appropriately safeguard patient information; failure to document training of employees on policies and procedures in the HIPAA Privacy and Security Rules; failure to identify a security official and conduct a risk analysis; and failure to obtain BAAs with internet-based email and calendar services where the provision of the service included storage and access to its ePHI.

North Carolina clinic pays $750,000 for failing to execute a BAA[16]

An orthopedic clinic in North Carolina agreed to pay $750,000 to settle HIPAA violation charges after an investigation found that the group did not enter into a BAA with a potential business partner before providing the partner with access to the PHI of 17,300 patients in 2013. The settlement included the monetary payment and corrective action.

Texas cancer center fined $4,348,000 for data breaches from unencrypted ePHI[17]

In 2018, a University of Texas cancer center was ordered to pay $4,348,000 in civil penalties for HIPAA violations related to the organization's encryption policies. An OCR investigation found that although the entity had identified unencrypted ePHI as a high risk and had developed encryption policies, the policies were never implemented. The theft of an unencrypted laptop and loss of two USB drives compromised the ePHI of over 33 thousand patients.

---

14 https://www.justice.gov/usao-ma/pr/springfield-doctor-convicted-jury-illegally-sharing-patient-medical-files

15 https://www.hhs.gov/hipaa/for-professionals/compliance-enforcement/examples/phoenix-cardiac-surgery/index.html

16 https://www.hhs.gov/hipaa/for-professionals/compliance-enforcement/agreements/raleigh-orthopaedic-clinic-bulletin/index.html

17 https://www.hhs.gov/about/news/2018/06/18/judge-rules-in-favor-of-ocr-and-requires-texas-cancer-center-to-pay-4.3-million-in-penalties-for-hipaa-violations.html

Healthcare company agrees to pay $3.5 million after reporting breach incidents by five of its CEs[18]

A Massachusetts-based healthcare company agreed to pay a $3.5 million fine after reporting data breaches at five of its sites in 2012. The company, which provides products and services to patients with kidney conditions, also agreed to adopt a comprehensive corrective action plan after an OCR investigation revealed that the CE had not conducted an adequate risk analysis to identify vulnerabilities to its ePHI.

Florida hospital operator pays $5.5 million HIPAA settlement for unauthorized employee access to PHI[19]

A non-profit corporation in Florida that operates hospitals, an urgent care center, a nursing home and other healthcare facilities agreed to settle HIPAA violation claims with a $5.5 million payment in 2017. The CE reported to OCR that two employees had impermissibly accessed the PHI of 115,143 patients and disclosed it to affiliated physician office staff. A second breach occurred when the login credentials of a former employee of an affiliated physician's office had been used to access the ePHI daily without detection from April 2011 to April 2012, affecting 80,000 individuals. The investigation found that although the CE had workforce access policies and procedures in place, the entity failed to implement procedures with respect to reviewing, modifying and/or terminating users' right of access, and failed to regularly review records of information system activity on applications that maintain electronic protected health information by workforce users and users at affiliated physician practices.

---

[18] https://www.hhs.gov/about/news/2018/02/01/five-breaches-add-millions-settlement-costs-entity-failed-heed-hipaa-s-risk-analysis-and-risk.html

[19] https://www.hhs.gov/about/news/2017/02/16/hipaa-settlement-shines-light-on-the-importance-of-audit-controls.html

Chapter 8

HIPAA Violations

Overview

In this chapter, you will learn how HIPAA violations occur and how they impact patients and entities. You will also learn how to manage a HIPAA complaint from a patient, and how to handle suspected breaches.

Chapter Outline

8.1 How HIPAA violations happen
8.2 How HIPAA violations impact patients
8.3 How HIPAA violations impact healthcare providers
8.4 HIPAA breaches
8.5 Handling a patient HIPAA complaint
8.6 Reporting noncompliance
8.7 Handling a cyberattack
8.8 Breach by a Business Associate

Learning Objectives

After completing this chapter, you should be able to do the following:

- ✓ Understand how and why privacy and security violations occur.
- ✓ Explain how HIPAA violations impact the patient and the CE.
- ✓ Learn how to manage patient complaints and internal reports of noncompliance.
- ✓ Address cyberattacks and breaches by Business Associates.

It's no secret that healthcare providers frequently struggle with HIPAA requirements, and it is a fact that HIPAA compliance can be complex, time-consuming, and costly. Some healthcare providers argue that the regulations get in the way of patient care.

PHI confidentiality, integrity, and availability are critical to quality care and a successful healthcare operation.

But PHI is the lifeblood of every healthcare entity. Patients come to their caregivers for treatment, and caregivers record those interactions in order to provide good care and to successfully run their businesses. That data is what fuels both the CE's mission and its business model. Therefore, it only makes sense to take any measures necessary to protect this precious resource.

Healthcare providers are also patients. When providers are asked to stop and think about their own healthcare needs, their own PHI, and how they would feel if their confidential medical information were made public, or if they found themselves the victims of identity theft, providers invariably temper their criticism. They too appreciate the protections afforded them by HIPAA.

Finally, while HIPAA compliance requires significant investment, a healthcare system without HIPAA would arguably require even more. For example, one of HIPAA's stated missions is to promote standards that make sharing ePHI easier and less expensive; although this is a daunting task in a world where technology is evolving so rapidly, the goal continues to be significant cost savings and more efficient operations for CEs, and more manageable costs for patients. In addition, HIPAA violations can be wildly expensive. Not just the fines, but the damage control and the lasting harm to the CE's business and reputation, and to the patients' lives.

8.1 How HIPAA Violations Happen

CEs can't lock PHI up behind impenetrable walls and leave it there. PHI must be allowed to circulate if healthcare entities are to operate and patients are to receive care. That is why HIPAA addresses permitted uses and disclosures (see Section 2.5) and requires CEs to make PHI available for those uses and disclosures.

In other words, the walls need doors to let PHI in and out. And those doors need locks.

HIPAA Privacy and Security administrative requirements provide guidance for the "locks"—the practices that CEs can use to keep PHI safe. (See Chapters 4 and 5.) This chapter takes a closer look at ways the locks can fail, that is, the risks to the privacy and security of PHI.

HIPAA violations refer to instances where PHI has been improperly used or disclosed. The use or disclosure may be unintentional, the result of an error, or it may be a deliberate crime. It may be the result of an unsecured facility, an indiscreet employee, or an unscrupulous cybercriminal.

Below are a few of the ways that PHI can be compromised, which can lead to investigations, fines, and to exposed patients. Reflecting on such examples is typically the first step that healthcare providers take when conducting a risk assessment of their operations in order to develop and implement a HIPAA compliance plan.

Examples of mishandled medical records and HIPAA authorizations:

- Information is released on the wrong patient.
- Information is released to an unauthorized party.
- Written consent or authorization is not secured before releasing PHI not covered by HIPAA permitted uses and disclosures.
- A record with an invalid or expired authorization is released.
- A patient requests to have PHI emailed to him or her, and the PHI is sent to the patient without first notifying him or her that the PHI is not encrypted.
- PHI is disclosed for a subpoena that does not meet Privacy Rule requirements.
- A minor's PHI is used or disclosed without the parent or guardian's consent.

Examples of improper office practices:

- Patient charts or records are left out on a desk or in an exam room where they can be seen by other patients not authorized to see them.
- Healthcare providers don't take reasonable safeguards to address facility characteristics (for example, an open floor plan or a pharmacy counter in a supermarket) when discussing PHI with patients.
- Medical records are left in unlocked rooms or cabinets.
- Paper records are tossed into the regular trash without being shredded or otherwise destroyed.

- Staff are not properly trained on HIPAA policies and procedures.

Examples of vulnerable facilities:

- A computer is left unattended in an accessible area with unsecured PHI.
- Computers with access to PHI remain logged in or are not password-protected.
- Office doors that are supposed to be locked are left unlocked.
- Office visitors or service people are allowed to move around the office unsupervised.
- Medical records are stored where they can be damaged or lost in a fire, flood, or other accident or natural disaster.

Examples of employee indiscretions:

- Employees discuss patient information in public areas.
- Employees discuss patient information with friends, family, community members, or co-workers.
- Employees post photos or information containing PHI on social media.
- Employees access patient records from home devices or mobile devices where it can be seen or accessed by others.
- Minimum necessary requirements are not followed, resulting in employees having access to more PHI than they need to do their jobs.

Tips for all forms of social media usage

- Make sure employees understand not to post anything that could not be said in another setting (like the crowded elevator). It is best if employees refrain from commenting about their workday online in any way.
- Do not allow pictures in the workplace to be posted online or have a policy that requires prior approval to prevent the unintentional exposure of PHI.
- Remind employees to use caution if responding to medical questions in a social media setting because they may inadvertently reveal PHI.

Appendix B contains a sample Social Media Policy.

Insider threats:

- An employee accesses PHI on a friend or family out of curiosity.
- An employee accesses PHI for personal gain, revenge, or extortion.
- An employee sells PHI to bad actors seeking to leverage the information.

Unprotected ePHI:

- A non-encrypted, non-password-protected laptop, desktop, tablet, memory stick, or other electronic device is lost or stolen.
- Unsecured ePHI is texted or emailed.
- ePHI can be accessed without a password.

Cybercrime:

- Inadequate technical safeguards expose the CE to a cyberattack that results in the loss, theft or destruction of ePHI.

8.2 How HIPAA Violations Impact Patients

It is difficult to overstate the devastating consequences that can result when a patient's privacy has been violated. Patients who have been the victims of privacy violations have reported losing their jobs; becoming estranged from friends, family, or their community; having their reputations damaged; even becoming the targets of blackmail. Privacy violations can also result in identity theft, which can require arduous and costly measures to resolve.

Confidentiality is also essential for providing effective care to patients. Patients who do not trust their healthcare provider to keep their personal information confidential will be hesitant to reveal information about themselves or family members for fear that it could leak out. This lack of trust interferes with medical care, because a patient might opt to hold back critical details that the caregiver needs to effectively treat the patient.

Patients who believe that their PHI has been compromised have the right to file a complaint with HHS (see Sections 3.5 and 8.5). HIPAA does not give patients the right to sue for damages in the event of a privacy violation. However, patients may be successful in pursuing other legal avenues at the state level, such as suing for invasion of privacy, breach of contract, or breach of doctor-patient confidentiality. This is easier in some states than in others—lawsuits filed in state courts have used HIPAA standards to establish liability.

Connecticut Supreme Court rules confidentiality between physicians and their patients is a common law of duty

In January 2018, the Connecticut Supreme Court ruled that patients recognized the patient's right to sue for unauthorized disclosure of medical information.

The decision stemmed from a 2004 lawsuit brought by a patient against her obstetric practice for releasing her medical records without authorization. Emily Byrne was treated at Avery Center for Obstetrics & Gynecology during her pregnancy, and gave explicit instructions that her medical records not be shared with Andro Mendoza, a man she had been in a relationship with. Mendoza filed a paternity action and his attorney served a subpoena on Avery for Byrne's medical records.

Rather than comply with HIPAA before disclosing PHI, Avery opted to provide the plaintiff's medical file to Mendoza's attorney. (See Section 2.5.2.1.5 on subpoenas.)

Mendoza reviewed the entire file and, according to Byrne, used the information to harass and extort Byrne and family. Byrne filed lawsuit against provider alleging that she suffered emotional distress due to disclosure.

The case was appealed many times until 2018, when the state's Supreme Court ruled that "recognizing a cause of action for the breach of the duty of confidentiality in the physician-patient relationship by the disclosure of medical information is not barred."[20]

HIPAA does not allow an individual to sue a provider for failing to comply with HIPAA, only to file a complaint with OCR. However, in this case, the court found that HIPAA creates a standard of care that can be used to show a duty of confidentiality between patient and provider, which could provide patients with a solid argument if they decide to sue for a privacy breach. Other state courts have allowed similar cases to be filed by patients on the basis that the privacy rights under HIPAA create a standard of care.

8.3 How HIPAA Violations Impact Healthcare Providers

The repercussions of noncompliance and privacy violations for CEs, BAs, and other entities required to comply with HIPAA can be equally damaging.

Even if an entity has not experienced a privacy violation, if a random compliance audit by the OCR uncovers examples of noncompliance, it could lead to further investigation and may possibly lead to a corrective action plan. This would require the entity to design and implement a plan that complies with HIPAA standards (which it should have already done) under the watchful eye of the OCR and typically on a tight deadline. Corrective action plans can include the following:

- ePHI risk analysis

[20] *Emily Byrne v. Avery Ctr. for Obstetrics & Gynecology, P.C.*, 327 Conn. 540, (2018).

- ePHI encryption
- Documentation of privacy, security, and breach notification policies and procedures
- Workforce training

Retroactively implementing or shoring up a HIPAA compliance plan can be disruptive and costly. In addition, even though a breach did not occur, the OCR may impose fines on the company for noncompliance (HIPAA enforcement and penalties are discussed in detail in Chapter 7.) The types of noncompliance resulting in such fines include failure to maintain proper security documentation, failure to train the workforce on privacy and security practices, and failure to have a BAA in place with BAs.

If the OCR investigates a privacy violation complaint and finds that a patient's PHI has actually been violated, it may impose a substantial fine on the company, based on how serious the violation and the entity's knowledge of the noncompliance that led to the violation. Fines increase significantly if more than one violation occurs in the same calendar year.

In addition to fines levied by the OCR, state attorneys general can issue their own HIPAA fines. Add to that the money that the entity will have to spend to defend itself against charges of HIPAA violations and to correct any noncompliant areas.

Employees involved in a HIPAA violation can also be held liable for the breach. If an employee is found to have compromised a patient's medical privacy by accessing the records without authority or for no medical reason, that employee can be fired, lose their medical license, fined, and even spend time in jail.

Finally, an entity found to have violated patient privacy risks serious damage to its reputation, and, as a result, business losses.

8.4 HIPAA Breaches

From 2009 to 2017, HHS recorded 2,181 healthcare data breaches involving more than 500 records that affected a total of nearly 177 million healthcare records.

In 2018, 229 data breaches affecting 6.1 million individuals had been reported to the OCR's breach portal through August 2018. Of these, 91 were listed as hacking/IT incidents impacting 4.3 million individuals—70 percent of the year's victims to date. Another 91 incidents were listed as unauthorized access/disclosure breaches, impacting nearly 803,000 individuals, and 41 were listed as theft or loss (affecting 677,000 individuals, 13 of which involved paper or film records). Six involved improper disposal (affecting 330,000 individuals), and the remainder involved unencrypted computing devices (affecting 80,000 individuals).

OCR Breach Reporting Tool

OCR maintains a website called the HIPAA Breach Reporting Tool (HBRT), unofficially known as the "Wall of Shame," where it publishes a list of entities that have experienced breaches that have affected 500 or more people.

The HBRT was mandated by the 2009 HITECH Act. Information on the site includes:

- The entity's name
- The state where the entity is located
- The date of the breach
- The type of breach (e.g., hacking/IT incident, theft, loss, unauthorized access/disclosure)
- The location of the breached information (e.g., laptop, paper records, desktop computer)
- The number of individuals affected by the breach

In 2017, the OCR made changes to the HBRT to help site users identify recent healthcare data breaches more quickly and to learn how breaches are investigated and resolved. Site features include:

- Breaches currently under investigation and reported within the last 24 months
- An archive of older breaches with information about how breaches were resolved
- Improved navigation to additional breach information
- Tips for consumers

The HBRT can be found at: https://ocrportal.hhs.gov/ocr/breach/breach_report.jsf

8.5 Handling a Patient HIPAA Complaint

An entity may learn of a breach concern from a patient. If a patient brings a privacy violation concern to a CE, it is critical for the entity to address the complaint immediately in order to reduce the risk of exposure. The following steps can help effectively address the complaint and mitigate risks.

- **Provide the patient with clear instructions for filing a complaint.** The CE must provide patients with instructions and mechanisms for filing a HIPAA complaint, such as completing a complaint form. Upon receiving the complaint, the privacy officer, or other designated person(s), must take over to investigate and determine whether a HIPAA breach has occurred. NOTE: The entity should be careful to avoid any action that could be construed as retaliating against the patient for filing the complaint.

- **Respond quickly to the complaint.** Treat all patient complaints of privacy seriously by taking prompt action. The HIPAA Breach Notification Rule (See Chapter 6) provides entities with guidance to determine whether a breach has occurred, and steps to take if a breach is confirmed. Also, take immediate action to stop a suspected breach. For example, stop improper access to PHI; make efforts to get back PHI that was improperly disclosed; and obtain assurances from recipients that they have not, or will not, further use or disclose improperly accessed PHI. Any actions taken should be carefully documented.

Quick response to a HIPAA violation complaint is important to address possible issues quickly and effectively.

- **Conduct an investigation.** To determine whether a breach has occurred, the entity must engage in fact-finding and root cause analysis. The entity must follow its established policies and procedures to investigate the nature and extent of the PHI involved, and workforce members who were involved in the incident must be identified and interviewed, and must provide written statements. The investigation should also be used identify the cause of the breach and help determine ways to prevent similar breaches in the future.
- **Correct and mitigate harmful effects of the complaint.** If the investigation confirms a breach has occurred, HIPAA requires the entity to mitigate the harmful effects of the breach. Entities should implement the mitigation plan developed to take all actions necessary to stop further disclosure or uses of unauthorized PHI and mitigate the harmful effects of unauthorized use or disclosure. Mitigation efforts may include updating policies and procedures, providing refresher compliance training for staff, and/or implementing new safeguards to prevent noncompliance.
- **Determine whether and how the breach must be reported.** If an investigation indicates there is more than a low probability that unsecured PHI has been breached, the breach will need to be reported according to the Breach Notification Rule (see Chapter 6).
- **Work with Human Resources to determine disciplinary measures.** HIPAA requires entities to sanction employees who violate HIPAA (see Sections 4.5 and 6.3). The compliance officer should work with human resources staff to review the sanctions policy and determine the appropriate disciplinary measures to take.

- **Document all actions.** CEs should make sure to follow their policies and procedures for addressing a patient complaint, and must document all actions taken. This includes all steps described here: the patient complaint; the internal investigation; confirmation that a breach occurred, or, rationale for concluding that no breach occurred; documents reviewed and witness statements obtained; actions taken to mitigate the breach; breach notification actions; and disciplinary actions.
- **Follow up with the patient.** The patient has a right to know the outcome of his or her complaint. The compliance officer or appointed designee should notify the patient of the findings of the investigation and how the complaint was resolved.

Learn from the experience

If a patient alerts you to a potential problem, act swiftly and proactively. Also take this opportunity to review your compliance program and make changes to ensure that your entity is prepared to prevent, detect, and resolve HIPAA issues.

8.6 Reporting Noncompliance

It is possible for an entity to discover HIPAA noncompliance that does not result from a complaint or an OCR review. The discovery may stem from a suspected breach, or from a risk analysis, or from a periodic review of policies and procedures.

In these cases, the first line of defense is an informed and invested workforce. Employees who are properly trained to recognize noncompliance or potential breaches and take immediate steps can be valuable assets in getting the situation more quickly in hand and limiting PHI exposure.

If an employee suspects either a breach or non-compliance, he or she should report the incident **immediately** to the designated compliance officer, with full confidence that there will be no retaliation for making the report.

The compliance officer must act quickly to investigate the employee's concerns. If the officer even suspects a breach has occurred, he or she should operate under the assumption that there has in fact been a breach, unless the circumstances meet one of the breach exceptions. The subsequent investigation will determine next steps.

The 7 Steps to Address a HIPAA Complaint

Timely Respond to Patient Complaints

The clock is ticking if there is a breach of PHI. Penalties can be avoided/reduced if corrected within

30 DAYS

Conduct an Adequate Investigation

Correct and Mitigate Harmful Effects

Determine if there is a Reportable Breach

Do not report if an exception applies:

- Unintentional access that does not result in further use or disclosure that violates HIPAA.
- An inadvertent disclosure of PHI
- Good faith belief that the unauthorized person would not likely retain the PHI

Report the breach If there is more than a low probability of PHI compromise based on a risk assessment of the 4 factors:

- The nature and extent of the PHI involved, including the types of identifiers and the likelihood of re-identification
- The unauthorized person who used the PHI or to whom the disclosure was made
- Whether the PHI was actually acquired or viewed
- The extent to which the risk to the PHI has been mitigated

Involve HR to Determine Disciplinary Measures

HIPAA requires covered entities to sanction employees who violate HIPAA. Work with HR to identify the appropriate disciplinary measures to take.

Document and Record all Investigative Efforts

Follow up with the Patient

Notify the patient of the findings and resolution of their complaint.

Click the link below for a sample HIPAA Privacy Complaint Form.

8.7 Handling a Cyberattack

As noted in section 8.4, cyberattacks were responsible for the 70 percent of victims affected by HIPAA breaches from January to August 2018.

Cyberattacks refer to a deliberate attack on computers, computer systems, or computer networks. Bad actors use malicious code to disrupt activity and access information for nefarious purposes, including identity theft, fraud, and extortion.

The Security Rule provides entities with guidance to help safeguard ePHI from unauthorized access, use, or disclosure as a result of cyberattack, which includes training employees to recognize and resist social engineering cyberattacks such as phishing, vishing, whaling, cyber-extortion, and ransomware, as well as other practices that could provide bad actors with access to computer networks, such as password practices, log off practices, use of USB drives etc.

If cybercriminals have successfully breached confidential patient data, an entity must take quick and decisive action to stop the attack and mitigate the harm. HHS provides the following recommendations to entities that have experienced a cyberattack or similar cybersecurity incident:

Entities must implement the response and mitigation procedures and contingency plans that they have developed according to the Security Rule's Administrative Safeguards (see Sections 5.4.6 and 5.4.7). For example, the entity should immediately identify and repair the source of the security incident, and it should take steps to mitigate any unauthorized use or disclosure of PHI. This can be done by the entity's internal IT staff, or, the entity can work with an outside contractor to address the issue. Because the incident involves PHI, the contractor would likely be a BA, so the entity would need to make sure to formalize the relationship with a BAA.

HHS recommends that entities that have suffered a cyberattack report the crime to other law enforcement agencies. This could include state or local police, the Federal Bureau of Investigation (FBI), and/or the Secret Service. Note: the entity should not include PHI in reports to law enforcement agencies, unless permitted by the HIPAA Privacy Rule. If a law enforcement official informs the entity that reporting a potential breach could interfere with a criminal investigation or could harm national security, the entity must wait to report the breach. The law enforcement

official may provide a date that the entity can report the incident; if the official asks for the delay orally, the entity should make the report after 30 days have passed.

HHS recommends that entities also report cyber security incidents to federal and information-sharing and analysis organizations (ISAOs), including the Department of Homeland Security, the HHS Assistant Secretary for Preparedness and Response, and private-sector cyber-threat ISAOs. Again, entities should not include PHI.

The entity is required to follow the Breach Notification Rule (see Chapter 6), including notifying OCR (OCR does not receive cybersecurity incident reports from federal agencies or HHS).

In addition to helping resolve the cyberattack, such measures will be favorably considered by OCR when it investigates the incident. OCR considers all mitigation efforts taken by the entity, including voluntary reporting of breach-related incidents with law enforcement agencies and other federal and analysis organizations.

Mitigating risk: Cyber liability insurance

Although cyber liability insurance is not required by HIPAA, many healthcare companies opt to purchase policies to manage the risk of ePHI breaches. Such policies, typically cover liability and property loss that results from a breach.

The policies can cover a variety of expenses associated with data breaches, including: notification costs, credit monitoring, costs to defend claims by state regulators, fines and penalties, and loss resulting from identity theft.

They may also cover property exposures from business interruption, data loss/destruction, computer fraud, funds transfer loss, and cyber extortion.

In the event of a healthcare data breach, a policy may cover forensic analysis, public relations, patient notification, regulatory fines, or even liability to third parties.

When considering a policy, an entity should carefully assess its needs and potential risks to ensure that the policy meets its requirements.

8.8 Business Associate Breaches

In 2015, a single breach by a BA in Indiana affected more than 3.9 million individuals. The BA, an electronic medical record services provider, discovered that hackers had gained access three weeks before the attack was discovered. Exposed ePHI included names, phone numbers, mailing addresses, user names, hashed passwords, security questions and answers, email addresses, birthdates, Social Security numbers, lab results, health insurance policy information, diagnoses, disability codes, doctors' names, medical conditions, and spouses' and children's names and birthdates.

In December 2018, twelve states filed a federal lawsuit against the BA claiming the BA violated HIPAA and other state regulations by failing to implement adequate security measures and not encrypting the ePHI.

Under the Omnibus Rule, BAs are directly liable for ePHI breaches (see Section 1.3). CEs are required to have a written agreement in place that addresses how the BA will protect PHI. (See Section 5.7.1.1.)

If a CE discovers that a BA is not fulfilling the terms of the BAA, the CE must take reasonable steps to ensure that the BA complies with the agreement, and, if necessary, end the relationship with the BA. If for some reason the CE cannot terminate the contract with the BA, it must report the problem to the OCR.

A CE that fails to address a BA's failure to comply with the BAA is considered to be out of compliance with the Privacy Rule, and is not permitted to make any further PHI disclosures to the BA. In cases where a CE is also a BA, the CE is considered to be out of compliance with the Privacy Rule if it violates the satisfactory assurances it provided as a BA of another CE.

OCR recommends CEs to take the following precautions regarding BAs and breaches when drafting a BAA:

A comprehensive business associate agreement tailored specifically to the relationship with the CE is a valuable compliance tool.

- The BAA should define how any PHI shared with the BA will be used or disclosed by the BA. The BAA should stipulate that the BA is to report to the CE any instances where it used or disclosed PHI for purposes not included in the BAA. Such uses and disclosures include unsecured PHI breaches and security incidents.
- The BAA should include a timeframe for BAs and their subcontractors to report a breach, security incident, or cyber-attack.
- The BAA should include the type of information that the BA or subcontractor would need to provide in a breach or security incident report.
- CEs and BAs should train workforce members on incident reporting and conduct security audits and assessments to evaluate the BAs' or subcontractors' security and privacy practices.

In the event of a breach, a BA must report the incident immediately to the CE impacted by the breach. As part of the written BA agreement, the CE may require the BA to notify the affected individuals, notify the OCR via its portal, alert the media in the case of a larger breach and cover any costs that result from the breach, such as credit monitoring. (See Section 6.2.4 for BA notification requirements.)

Chapter 9

HIPAA Compliance Checklist

Overview

This chapter provides a checklist that can be used as for developing and implementing a HIPAA compliance plan, or as a way to review a plan already in place.

The checklist addresses the administrative requirements for the Privacy Rule and Security Rule, as well as considerations for reporting breaches.

This checklist is not designed to be a comprehensive compliance plan. Rather, it is a starting point to help healthcare providers think about some of the specific risks that might jeopardize PHI privacy and security, and some of the measures that can be taken to address HIPAA requirements.

9.1 Privacy Policies and Procedures

Activity	✓
CEs must review their privacy policies and procedures periodically to ensure that they are consistent, complete and up-to-date in order to ensure HIPAA compliance.	
Privacy policies and procedures should include a process for documenting actions, assessments, communications, and designations required by the Privacy Rule.	
The privacy official responsible for the development, maintenance, and implementation of privacy policies and procedures should be designated in writing.	
The privacy official is responsible for ensuring that the CE's workforce is properly trained, and that all training is documented.	

9.2 Security Policies and Procedures

Activity	✓
CEs must review their security policies and procedures periodically to ensure that they are complete and up-to-date in order to ensure HIPAA compliance, and must document every change made to the security policies and procedures.	
Security policies and procedures are to include a process for documenting actions, activities, assessments, communications, and designations required by the Security Rule.	
The designated security official is responsible for the development, maintenance, and implementation of HIPAA policies and procedures.	
The security official is responsible for ensuring that the CE's workforce who handle ePHI is properly trained, and that all training is documented.	

9. 3 Breach Notification Policies and Procedures

Activity	✓
Entities must have procedures in place to quickly assess whether a suspected breach event has resulted in the compromise of PHI.	
Entities must have procedures in place to notify affected individuals, the media, and HHS if they determine that unsecured PHI has been compromised in accordance with the Breach Notification Rule.	
CEs should address the breach notification process in agreements with BAs.	
Entities must document all breach notification activity; if an entity determines that an incident did not constitute a breach, or that PHI was not compromised, it must document how that conclusion was reached.	

9.4 Organizational Boundaries

Activity	✓
An important component of privacy policies and procedures is drafting a written document to clarify organizational boundaries for the CE, including BAs. This essentially means to determine how to separate out the different operations, or components, of an entity and build walls between them so that PHI can be contained. For purposes of PHI privacy, employees of one component should treat members of another component as though they are employees of a separate entity.	
If an employee has responsibilities in more than one component, the CE must take measures to ensure that the employee does not use or disclose PHI created or received in one component while working in another.	

9.5 BA Contracts

As part of the compliance plan, CEs must carefully track and document relationships with BAs. A CE must have up-to-date written contracts (BA Agreements) that meet all current HIPAA requirements.

HIPAA Rules generally require that CEs enter into contracts with their BAs to ensure that the BAs will appropriately safeguard PHI. BAs must similarly enter into contracts with their subcontractors when their subcontractors also fall under the definition of a BA.

A written contract between a CE and a BA must:

Activity	✓
Establish the permitted and required uses and disclosures of protected health information by the BA.	
Provide that the BA will not use or further disclose the information other than as permitted or required by the contract or as required by law.	
Require the BA to implement appropriate safeguards to prevent unauthorized use or disclosure of the information, including implementing requirements of the HIPAA Security Rule with regard to electronic protected health information.	
Require the BA to report to the CE any use or disclosure of the information not provided for by its contract, including incidents that constitute breaches of unsecured protected health information.	
Require the BA to disclose protected health information as specified in its contract to satisfy a CE's obligation with respect to individuals' requests for copies of their protected health information, as well as make available protected health information for amendments (and incorporate any amendments, if required) and accountings.	
To the extent the BA is to carry out a CE's obligation under the Privacy Rule, require the BA to comply with the requirements applicable to the obligation.	
Require the BA to make available to HHS its internal practices, books, and records relating to the use and disclosure of protected health information received from, or created or received by the BA on behalf of, the CE for purposes of HHS determining the CE's compliance with the HIPAA Privacy Rule.	
At termination of the contract, if feasible, require the BA to return or destroy all protected health information received from, or created or received by the BA on behalf of, the CE.	
Require the BA to ensure that any subcontractors it may engage on its behalf that will have access to protected health information agree to the same restrictions and conditions that apply to the BA with respect to such information.	
Authorize termination of the contract by the CE if the BA violates a material term of the contract. Contracts between BAs and BAs that are subcontractors are subject to these same requirements.	

9.6 HIPAA-Related Documents

Activity	✓
CEs must retain all documentation related HIPAA compliance for 6 years from the date of creation or the date when it last was in effect, whichever is later.	
HIPAA-related documents should be reviewed and updated to respond to environmental or operational changes that may affect the security of ePHI.	

9.7 Training and Enforcement

Activity	✓
All employees, including management, must be trained on HIPAA within a reasonable time of their hire to keep them current on updated policies and procedures and all training should be documented. Additional training should be given to employees any time a change in policies and procedures affects their role and responsibilities. The training program should include tools to verify that employees understand and are complying with policies and procedures.	
Training must include a program on identifying and responding to a potential breach of PHI.	
In addition to training, an ongoing security awareness program for all employees, including management, is an effective tool to keep the importance of security top of mind and to alert employees about the latest security issues.	
Appropriate sanctions against those who fail to comply with HIPAA policies and procedures should be applied promptly and consistently, and all sanctions should be documented.	

9.8 Limiting Access to PHI

Activity	✓
The minimum necessary standard requires CEs to evaluate their practices and enhance safeguards as needed to limit unnecessary or inappropriate access to and disclosure of PHI.	
Some CEs have made the mistake of trying to simplify HIPAA efforts by providing all employees with PHI access, but this can result in bigger problems later on. Instead, CEs should make reasonable efforts to limit the number of individuals with access, and clearly articulate and limit the categories of PHI to which they have access.	

9.9 Limiting Access to ePHI

Activity	✓
The policies and procedures regarding security should include a decision process to determine whether or not a workforce member should have access to ePHI, as well as procedures for granting access to that person, such that the access is consistent with that person's need to work with ePHI. Users' right of access to specific workstations, transactions, programs, or processes should be clearly established, documented, reviewed, and modified as needed. In addition, when an employee leaves the organization or has a change in responsibilities, their access to ePHI should be terminated or limited/expanded as appropriate (Administrative safeguard).	
CEs and their BAs must implement policies and procedures for electronic information systems that maintain ePHI to allow access only to those persons or software programs that have been granted access in accordance with your authorization procedures. The procedures should include measures to prevent employees from accessing ePHI beyond their authorized level. (Technical safeguard).	

9.10 Passwords and Keycards

Activity	✓
Security and privacy policies and procedures should address creating, changing, and safeguarding passwords.	
Staff members should be given unique passwords according to their system access authorization, and training should include clear messages prohibiting employees from sharing passwords or keeping them written down near the computer. Policies and procedures should also include assigning a unique name and/or number for identifying and tracking user identity.	

9.11 Facility Precautions

CE should take these steps to address access to facilities:

Activity	✓
Limit the personnel who have access to the facility and systems.	
Control and validate people's access to the facility based on their role or function, including visitors.	
Limit physical access to electronic information systems and the facilities in which they are housed, while ensuring that properly authorized access is allowed.	
Implement physical safeguards for all workstations that access ePHI to restrict access to authorized users.	

Develop a current written Facility Security Plan with policies and procedures to safeguard the facility and equipment from unauthorized physical access, tampering, and theft.	
Document repairs and modifications to the physical components of the facilities which are related to security, such as hardware, walls, doors, and locks.	
Specify the proper functions to be performed, the manner in which those functions are to be performed, and the physical attributes of the surroundings of a specific workstation (or class of workstation) that can access ePHI.	
Track the receipt and removal of hardware and electronic media that contain ePHI into and out of the facility, as well as the movement of these items within the facility.	
Draft and implement a written Contingency Operations Plan with procedures that allow facility access in the event of an emergency (to support of restoration of lost data under the Disaster Recovery Plan and Emergency Mode Operations Plan).	
Protect paper and electronic medical files from access by unauthorized personnel.	
Install printers and fax machines in a location that offers privacy, and configure the fax machine to make sure the "fax disclaimer" appears on every outgoing fax.	
Post signs to restrict access to particular areas.	
Post signs to remind employees about confidentiality.	

9.12 Office Equipment Precautions

Precautions should also be taken with office equipment. CEs should take a careful look at their facilities to address these questions:

Activity	✓
Can computer monitors be viewed by patients/visitors?	
Is the telephone answering machine placed where messages being retrieved can be heard by people who should not have access?	
Do all computers have screen savers activated?	
Are electronic procedures used that terminate an electronic session after a predetermined time of inactivity?	
Do all computer users log off when they physically leave their workstations?	
Does the email disclaimer appear on all outgoing email?	
Is the security system updated as necessary to maintain its effectiveness as technology advances?	
Is a record kept of the movements of hardware and electronic media, and any person responsible for any of it?	
Are there multiple printouts at printers?	
Is a fax log kept where it can be seen by patients/visitors/nonauthorized employees?	

Do staff members text patient information to physicians/providers?	

9.13 Staff Precautions

Activity	✓
Routine staff activities in healthcare provider environments must be scrutinized to ensure that PHI is not inadvertently disclosed to unauthorized people. When patients sign in, sign-in sheets should only ask for the patient's name, time of appointment, time of arrival, and doctor's name, and patient registration should be done in a discreet manner. Conversations between staff and patients/visitors should be conducted in a way that protects patients' PHI, to avoid other patients and visitors overhearing the reason for the patient's visit.	
Medical records and other patient information should not be visible to visitors and should not be left unattended. Patient files should be clearly labeled as confidential and turned face down when not in use, and medical charts outside of exam rooms should be turned inward to hide information.	
Documents should be properly shredded in a timely manner and staff must make sure that PHI is not visible in trash bins.	
CEs should limit the amount of information left on answering machines. For example, a CE could leave only its name, number and the minimum additional information necessary to confirm an appointment, or ask the individual to call back. Staff should make sure that the patient has given permission to leave messages on the answering machine before leaving a message. A CE can leave a limited message with a patient's family member or someone else who answers the phone, but should use professional judgment to make sure that leaving the message is the patient's best interests.	

9.14 Correspondence

Activity	✓
Care should be taken with written correspondence. For example, windowed envelopes should only display the patient's name and address, and post cards with appointment reminders should only contain the patient's name and address, the doctor's name, and the time and date of the appointment. All correspondence containing PHI must be marked as confidential.	
Any fees charged for providing copies of a patient's medical record must be reasonable and cost-based (includes only labor for copying, costs for supplies, labor for creating a summary or explanation of the PHI if the individual requests a summary or explanation, and required postage; administrative and other costs associated with outsourcing the function cannot be included in the fee).	

9.15 Limiting the Amount of PHI Used or Disclosed

Activity	✓
For routine PHI disclosures, policies and procedures must address how to determine how much PHI can be used or disclosed, and procedures for proper disclosure.	
Non-routine disclosures of PHI need their own criteria for limiting the PHI disclosed. Disclosure requests should be reviewed on an individual basis in accordance with that criteria.	
When requesting PHI from other CEs on a routine basis, care must be taken to limit requests to only the PHI necessary to accomplish the purpose. Establish criteria to limit non-routine requests to only the PHI necessary to accomplish the purpose, and review requests on an individual basis in accordance with that criteria.	
CEs should refrain from using, disclosing, or requesting entire medical records unless they are necessary to accomplish the purpose of the use, disclosure, or request.	

9.16 Notice of Privacy Practices

Activity	✓
All CEs must have an NPP that is in compliance with HIPAA requirements. The NPP should be reviewed periodically and updated to reflect changes in the organization and ensure that it continue to comply with HIPAA requirements. CEs should ensure consistency between policies and procedures and privacy practices stated within the NPP whenever changes are made to either document. Older NPP versions should be archived, along with any written acknowledgments of receipt of these notices.	
The NPP must be on display for patients and visitors, and employees should explain the notice when providing it to patients and visitors. The NPP should also be posted prominently on the entity's website.	
Keep paper copies of the NPP readily available to give to patients, including those who acknowledge receipt electronically.	

9.17 Complaints about Privacy Practices

Patients have the right under HIPAA to complain if they believe their PHI has been improperly disclosed. Take these steps to manage privacy complaints:

Activity	✓
Keep privacy complaint forms available for patients.	
Designate in writing the person responsible for receiving complaints about privacy and able to answer questions about the NPP.	
Document all complaints received, as well as how they were resolved.	

Train staff to ensure that no one in the organization intimidates, threatens, coerces, discriminates against, or retaliates against anyone who makes a complaint against the practice for its treatment of PHI. Document any cases of intimidation or retaliation, and take appropriate disciplinary measures stated in the policy and procedures.	
Never require an individual to waive the right to complain as a condition of treatment, payment, enrollment in a health plan, or eligibility for benefits.	

9.18 Authorization for Use or Disclosure of PHI

Activity	✓
Unless a use or disclosure is permitted or required by HIPAA without an authorization, the CE should refrain from using or disclosing PHI without an authorization that is valid under the law.	
CEs must inform an individual in advance of PHI disclosure for facility directories, including the persons to whom it may be disclosed, and give the individual an opportunity to agree to (or prohibit or restrict) the PHI use or disclosure.	
Proper authorization for PHI use or disclosure of PHI for marketing purposes or for sale of PHI is required.	
In an emergency, CEs should only disclose PHI if consistent with a prior expressed preference of the individual (if known) and in the individual's best interest.	
Use or disclosure must be consistent with a valid authorization.	
All signed authorizations must be documented and retained, and a copy of the signed document should be provided to the patient. In an emergency, CEs are only required to give patients notice when it is practical to do so, after the emergency has ended. In addition, where notice is delayed by an emergency treatment situation, the Privacy Rule does not require CEs to make a good faith effort to obtain the patient's written acknowledgment of receipt of the notice.	
Authorizations must be written in plain language.	

9. 19 Treatment of PHI

Activity	✓
CEs must implement a procedure to provide individuals with access to PHI and an accounting of PHI disclosures. They must also have procedures ready to implement to restrict uses and disclosures of PHI when requested to do so.	
CEs need a procedure in place to amend the PHI of an individual when requested to do so.	
CEs must ensure that they comply with all HIPAA requirements when de-identifying and re-identifying PHI.	
Data Use Agreements must comply with the HIPAA Privacy requirements.	
Fundraising communications must comply with the HIPAA Privacy requirements.	

9.20 Software

Activity	✓
All software must be HIPAA-compliant.	
CEs must implement procedures to control access to software programs for testing and revisions, as well as procedures for guarding against, detecting, and reporting malicious software.	

9.21 Computer Systems and ePHI (security)

CEs must have comprehensive policies and procedures in place to ensure that computer systems containing PHI are secure. CEs must:

Activity	✓
Maintain records of information system activity, such as audit logs, access reports, and security tracking reports.	
Implement hardware, software, and/or procedural mechanisms that record and examine activity in information systems that contain or use ePHI.	
Review information system activity records to identify inappropriate activity.	
Have procedures in place for monitoring log-in attempts and reporting discrepancies.	
Implement procedures to verify that a person or entity seeking access to ePHI is the one claimed.	
Implement policies and procedures to protect ePHI from improper alteration or destruction.	
Implement electronic mechanisms to corroborate that ePHI has not been altered or destroyed in an unauthorized manner.	
Implement security measures to ensure that ePHI is not being improperly modified during transmission without detection.	
Implement technical security measures to guard against unauthorized access to ePHI that is being transmitted over an electronic communications network.	
Implement a mechanism to encrypt and decrypt ePHI.	
Implement policies and procedures to address the final disposition of ePHI and/or the hardware or electronic media on which it is stored.	
Implement procedures for removal of ePHI from electronic media before the media are made available for re-use.	
Have a current written analysis that shows which of your specific applications and data are most critical to implementing your contingency plans.	

Have, and implement as needed, procedures for obtaining necessary ePHI during an emergency.	
Have current written policies and procedures for responding to an emergency or disaster that damages systems containing ePHI.	
Implement a backup plan with procedures to create and maintain retrievable exact copies of ePHI.	
Create a retrievable exact copy of ePHI as needed before moving any equipment.	
Have (and implement as necessary) a disaster recovery plan with procedures to restore any loss of data.	
Have (and implement as needed) an Emergency Mode Operation Plan with procedures to enable continuation of critical business processes that protect the security of ePHI while operating in emergency mode.	
Implement procedures for periodically testing and revising your contingency plans.	

9.22 Security Assessments and Analyses

Activity	✓
CEs should conduct periodic security assessments to determine whether reasonable procedures are in place to protect against threats to the security or integrity of ePHI, as well as procedures to protect against reasonably anticipated uses or disclosures of ePHI by unauthorized personnel.	
CE must conduct an accurate and thorough assessment of the potential risks and vulnerabilities to the confidentiality, integrity, and availability of ePHI held by the organization and its BAs, and take measures to reduce the risks and vulnerabilities found during risk analyses. Those measures should be periodically reviewed and tested (and modified as needed).	

9.23 Security Incidents

CEs should address all security incidents head on. Waiting to address an issue or attempting to conceal it will only exacerbate an already difficult situation. Detailed procedures should be developed and implemented to address suspected or known security incidents promptly. When developing and implementing policies and procedures, the following recommendations should be included:

Activity	✓
Implement procedures to identify and respond as needed to suspected or known security incidents, including breaches of unsecured PHI.	
Implement procedures as needed to mitigate harmful effects of security incidents that are known to the CE and BAs.	

Mitigate, to the extent practicable, any harmful effect known of a use or disclosure of PHI in violation of policies and procedures.	
Maintain documentation on security incidents that involve the CE or BAs, including their outcomes.	
Have a breach notification protocol in place.	
If any breaches involving 500 or more individuals, confirm that the breach notification protocol was followed. The protocol must include notifying all individuals potentially affected by the breach as well as the media and the Secretary of HHS.	
If any breaches involving fewer than 500 individuals occurred within the last calendar year, confirm that the breach notification protocol was followed, including notifying all individuals and informing the Secretary of HHS by February 28 of the following year.	
Ensure that if any BAs had a breach within the last year, they notified the CE as appropriate.	

Appendix A

Glossary of Terms

Term	Description
Business Associate (BA)	A person or entity that performs certain functions or activities that involve the use or disclosure of PHI on behalf of, or provides services to, a CE.
Business Associate Agreement (BAA)	A covered entity's contract or other written arrangement with its business associate.
Covered Entity (CE)	Health plans, healthcare clearinghouses, and healthcare providers that electronically transmit health information.
Department of Justice (DOJ)	Works in conjunction with the OCR on possible HIPAA criminal violations.
Department of Health and Human Services (HHS)	Administers HIPAA at the national level.
Designated Record Set (DRS)	A group of records maintained by or for a covered entity.
Electronic Data Inter-change (EDI)	The electronic transfer of medical, billing, and other HIPAA-covered information among CEs and BAs.
Electronic Health Record (EHR)	Electronic versions of patients' paper records kept by healthcare providers, such as medical history and physicians' notes; also known as Electronic Medical Records (EMR).
Electronic Protected Health Information (ePHI)	PHI that is stored and shared in electronic format.
Health Information Technology for Economic and Clinical Health Act (HITECH)	Created to stimulate the adoption of electronic health records (EHR) and the supporting technology in the United States.

Health Insurance Portability Act of 1996 (HIPAA)	Provides data privacy and security provisions for safeguarding medical information.
Hybrid Entity	An entity that performs some functions that are covered by HIPAA and other functions that are not.
Individually Identifiable Health Information (IIHI)	Health information that can be linked to a specific person, or could be used to identify a person; PHI is a subset of IIHI.
Non-covered entities (Non-CEs)	An entity that does not meet the definition of a covered entity or business associate, and does not have to comply with HIPAA.
Notice of Privacy Practices (NPP)	Provides a clear, user-friendly explanation of individuals' rights with respect to their personal health information and the privacy practices of CEs.
Office of Civil Rights (OCR)	An HHS agency responsible for enforcing the Privacy and Security Rules.
Omnibus Final Rule	A set of final regulations modifying the HIPAA Privacy, Security, and Enforcement Rules to implement various provisions of the HITECH Act.
Protected Health Information (PHI)	A subset of individually identifiable health information created or maintained by CEs and their BAs.
Treatment, Payment, and Healthcare Operations (TPO)	The HIPAA Privacy Rule permits CEs to use and disclose PHI, with certain limits and protections, for these routine, core healthcare activities.

Appendix B

Sample Documents

Notice of Privacy Practices Acknowledgment
(Practice Name)

I understand that under the Health Insurance Portability and Accountability Act (HIPAA), I have certain rights to privacy regarding my protected health information. I acknowledge that I have received or have been given the opportunity to receive a copy of your Notice of Privacy Practices. I also understand that this practice has the right to change its Notice of Privacy Practices and that I may contact the practice at any time to obtain a current copy of the Notice of Privacy Practices.

____ ____________________
Patient Name or Legal Guardian (print) Date

____
Signature

Office Use Only

We have made the following attempt to obtain the patient's signature acknowledging receipt of the Notice of Privacy Practices:

Date: ________________ Attempt: ____________________________________

Staff Name: ____

Request to Inspect or Copy Patient Information

Patient Name ____

Date of Birth ____

Patient Address ____
Street City, State, Zip

Date of Patient Request ______________

Requested patient information
(Please describe the information that you would like us to provide a copy of)

____
____
____

We will review your request to determine if the information can be made available to you. In some cases, we may be legally prohibited from disclosing certain information. For further details please refer to our Notice of Privacy Practice.

We will complete our review of your request within the next 30 days and contact you either by phone or in writing to arrange for you to inspect or pick up a copy of your records. An administrative fee of $________ will be charged for copying the requested material.

We will notify you if we are unable to accommodate or if we deny your request.

______________________________ ______________________
Patient Signature or Personal Representative Date

Office Use Only

Request was received by: ______________________________ Date __________
Name and title of staff receiving/processing this request

☐ We hereby accept the request.

____
Practice Representative (Type/Print)

☐ We hereby deny the request. ______________________________
Practice Representative Signature

Date __________

HIPAA Privacy Complaint Form

You may mail or fax this completed form to:
[Insert Mailing Address and fax]

You may also email the completed form to: *[Insert email address]*

Date: ____________________ Full Name: ____

Address: ____

Telephone Number: ________________________________ Email:_____________________________

Name of Patient: ____________________________ Relationship to Patient:_____________________
(if different from above)

Describe the complaint in detail, including the date of occurrence, the name(s) of any staff involved and other witnesses (attach additional sheets if necessary):

____

____

____

____

____

____

____

____

____

____

____ ______________________________
Patient or Legal Representative Signature Date

Internal Use
Date received: _________________________ Received by: ________________________________

Complaint delivered by (circle one): Email Mail Fax

Sample Business Associate Agreement Provisions[21]

Words or phrases contained in brackets are intended as either optional language or as instructions to the users of these sample provisions.

Definitions

Catch-all definition:

The following terms used in this Agreement shall have the same meaning as those terms in the HIPAA Rules: Breach, Data Aggregation, Designated Record Set, Disclosure, Health Care Operations, Individual, Minimum Necessary, Notice of Privacy Practices, Protected Health Information, Required By Law, Secretary, Security Incident, Subcontractor, Unsecured Protected Health Information, and Use.

Specific definitions:

a) Business Associate. "Business Associate" shall generally have the same meaning as the term "business associate" at 45 CFR 160.103, and in reference to the party to this agreement, shall mean [Insert Name of Business Associate].
b) Covered Entity. "Covered Entity" shall generally have the same meaning as the term "covered entity" at 45 CFR 160.103, and in reference to the party to this agreement, shall mean [Insert Name of Covered Entity].
c) HIPAA Rules. "HIPAA Rules" shall mean the Privacy, Security, Breach Notification, and Enforcement Rules at 45 CFR Part 160 and Part 164.

Obligations and Activities of Business Associate

Business Associate agrees to:

a) Not use or disclose protected health information other than as permitted or required by the Agreement or as required by law;
b) Use appropriate safeguards, and comply with Subpart C of 45 CFR Part 164 with respect to electronic protected health information, to prevent use or disclosure of protected health information other than as provided for by the Agreement;
c) Report to covered entity any use or disclosure of protected health information not provided for by the Agreement of which it becomes aware, including breaches of unsecured protected health information as required at 45 CFR 164.410, and any security incident of which it becomes aware;

   [The parties may wish to add additional specificity regarding the breach notification obligations of the business associate, such as a stricter timeframe for the business associate to report a potential breach to the covered entity and/or whether the business associate will handle

[21] https://www.hhs.gov/hipaa/for-professionals/covered-entities/sample-business-associate-agreement-provisions/index.html

breach notifications to individuals, the HHS Office for Civil Rights (OCR), and potentially the media, on behalf of the covered entity.]

d) In accordance with 45 CFR 164.502(e)(1)(ii) and 164.308(b)(2), if applicable, ensure that any subcontractors that create, receive, maintain, or transmit protected health information on behalf of the business associate agree to the same restrictions, conditions, and requirements that apply to the business associate with respect to such information;

e) Make available protected health information in a designated record set to the [Choose either "covered entity" or "individual or the individual's designee"] as necessary to satisfy covered entity's obligations under 45 CFR 164.524;

[The parties may wish to add additional specificity regarding how the business associate will respond to a request for access that the business associate receives directly from the individual (such as whether and in what time and manner a business associate is to provide the requested access or whether the business associate will forward the individual's request to the covered entity to fulfill) and the timeframe for the business associate to provide the information to the covered entity.]

f) Make any amendment(s) to protected health information in a designated record set as directed or agreed to by the covered entity pursuant to 45 CFR 164.526, or take other measures as necessary to satisfy covered entity's obligations under 45 CFR 164.526;

[The parties may wish to add additional specificity regarding how the business associate will respond to a request for amendment that the business associate receives directly from the individual (such as whether and in what time and manner a business associate is to act on the request for amendment or whether the business associate will forward the individual's request to the covered entity) and the timeframe for the business associate to incorporate any amendments to the information in the designated record set.]

g) Maintain and make available the information required to provide an accounting of disclosures to the [Choose either "covered entity" or "individual"] as necessary to satisfy covered entity's obligations under 45 CFR 164.528;

[The parties may wish to add additional specificity regarding how the business associate will respond to a request for an accounting of disclosures that the business associate receives directly from the individual (such as whether and in what time and manner the business associate is to provide the accounting of disclosures to the individual or whether the business associate will forward the request to the covered entity) and the timeframe for the business associate to provide information to the covered entity.]

h) To the extent the business associate is to carry out one or more of covered entity's obligation(s) under Subpart E of 45 CFR Part 164, comply with the requirements of Subpart E that apply to the covered entity in the performance of such obligation(s); and

i) Make its internal practices, books, and records available to the Secretary for purposes of determining compliance with the HIPAA Rules.

Permitted Uses and Disclosures by Business Associate

a) Business associate may only use or disclose protected health information

[Option 1 – Provide a specific list of permissible purposes.]

[Option 2 – Reference an underlying service agreement, such as "as necessary to perform the services set forth in Service Agreement."]

[In addition to other permissible purposes, the parties should specify whether the business associate is authorized to use protected health information to de-identify the information in accordance with 45 CFR 164.514(a)-(c). The parties also may wish to specify the manner in which the business associate will de-identify the information and the permitted uses and disclosures by the business associate of the de-identified information.]

b) Business associate may use or disclose protected health information as required by law.

c) Business associate agrees to make uses and disclosures and requests for protected health information.

[Option 1] consistent with covered entity's minimum necessary policies and procedures.

[Option 2] subject to the following minimum necessary requirements: [Include specific minimum necessary provisions that are consistent with the covered entity's minimum necessary policies and procedures.]

d) Business associate may not use or disclose protected health information in a manner that would violate Subpart E of 45 CFR Part 164 if done by covered entity [if the Agreement permits the business associate to use or disclose protected health information for its own management and administration and legal responsibilities or for data aggregation services as set forth in optional provisions (e), (f), or (g) below, then add ", except for the specific uses and disclosures set forth below."]

e) [Optional] Business associate may use protected health information for the proper management and administration of the business associate or to carry out the legal responsibilities of the business associate.

f) [Optional] Business associate may disclose protected health information for the proper management and administration of business associate or to carry out the legal responsibilities of the business associate, provided the disclosures are required by law, or business associate obtains reasonable assurances from the person to whom the information is disclosed that the information will remain confidential and used or further disclosed only as required by law or for the purposes for which it was disclosed to the person, and the person notifies business associate of any instances of which it is aware in which the confidentiality of the information has been breached.

g) [Optional] Business associate may provide data aggregation services relating to the health care operations of the covered entity.

Provisions for Covered Entity to Inform Business Associate of Privacy Practices and Restrictions

a) [Optional] Covered entity shall notify business associate of any limitation(s) in the notice of privacy practices of covered entity under 45 CFR 164.520, to the extent that such limitation may affect business associate's use or disclosure of protected health information.

b) [Optional] Covered entity shall notify business associate of any changes in, or revocation of, the permission by an individual to use or disclose his or her protected health information, to the extent that such changes may affect business associate's use or disclosure of protected health information.

c) [Optional] Covered entity shall notify business associate of any restriction on the use or disclosure of protected health information that covered entity has agreed to or is required to abide by under 45 CFR 164.522, to the extent that such restriction may affect business associate's use or disclosure of protected health information.

Permissible Requests by Covered Entity

[Optional] Covered entity shall not request business associate to use or disclose protected health information in any manner that would not be permissible under Subpart E of 45 CFR Part 164 if done by covered entity. [Include an exception if the business associate will use or disclose protected health information for, and the agreement includes provisions for, data aggregation or management and administration and legal responsibilities of the business associate.]

Term and Termination

a) Term. The Term of this Agreement shall be effective as of [Insert effective date], and shall terminate on [Insert termination date or event] or on the date covered entity terminates for cause as authorized in paragraph (b) of this Section, whichever is sooner.

b) Termination for Cause. Business associate authorizes termination of this Agreement by covered entity, if covered entity determines business associate has violated a material term of the Agreement [and business associate has not cured the breach or ended the violation within the time specified by covered entity]. [Bracketed language may be added if the covered entity wishes to provide the business associate with an opportunity to cure a violation or breach of the contract before termination for cause.]

c) Obligations of Business Associate Upon Termination.

[Option 1 – if the business associate is to return or destroy all protected health information upon termination of the agreement]

Upon termination of this Agreement for any reason, business associate shall return to covered entity [or, if agreed to by covered entity, destroy] all protected health information received from covered entity, or created, maintained, or received by business associate on behalf of covered entity, that the business associate still maintains in any form. Business associate shall retain no copies of the protected health information.

[Option 2—if the agreement authorizes the business associate to use or disclose protected health information for its own management and administration or to carry out its legal responsibilities and the business associate needs to retain protected health information for such purposes after termination of the agreement]

Upon termination of this Agreement for any reason, business associate, with respect to protected health information received from covered entity, or created, maintained, or received by business associate on behalf of covered entity, shall:

1. Retain only that protected health information which is necessary for business associate to continue its proper management and administration or to carry out its legal responsibilities;
2. Return to covered entity [or, if agreed to by covered entity, destroy] the remaining protected health information that the business associate still maintains in any form;

3. Continue to use appropriate safeguards and comply with Subpart C of 45 CFR Part 164 with respect to electronic protected health information to prevent use or disclosure of the protected health information, other than as provided for in this Section, for as long as business associate retains the protected health information;
4. Not use or disclose the protected health information retained by business associate other than for the purposes for which such protected health information was retained and subject to the same conditions set out at [Insert section number related to paragraphs (e) and (f) above under "Permitted Uses and Disclosures By Business Associate"] which applied prior to termination; and
5. Return to covered entity [or, if agreed to by covered entity, destroy] the protected health information retained by business associate when it is no longer needed by business associate for its proper management and administration or to carry out its legal responsibilities.

[The agreement also could provide that the business associate will transmit the protected health information to another business associate of the covered entity at termination, and/or could add terms regarding a business associate's obligations to obtain or ensure the destruction of protected health information created, received, or maintained by subcontractors.]

d) Survival. The obligations of business associate under this Section shall survive the termination of this Agreement.

Miscellaneous [Optional]

a) [Optional] Regulatory References. A reference in this Agreement to a section in the HIPAA Rules means the section as in effect or as amended.

b) [Optional] Amendment. The Parties agree to take such action as is necessary to amend this Agreement from time to time as is necessary for compliance with the requirements of the HIPAA Rules and any other applicable law.

c) [Optional] Interpretation. Any ambiguity in this Agreement shall be interpreted to permit compliance with the HIPAA Rules.

Blogging and Social Medial Policy

This Blogging and Social Media Policy applies to the personal conduct of all employees of the Employer while engaging in online conversations as representatives of the Employer. This policy focuses on avoiding the unique pitfalls online communication holds for professionals without restricting unnecessarily the ability of individual employees to be creative in taking advantage of technology. This policy applies to all forms of social media, including, but not limited to, blogs, video/photo posting sites, Wikipedia or other wikis, and social networking sites such as Facebook, Instagram, Twitter, and LinkedIn.

I. Blogging

Commenting on blogs should be done on personal time and employer issued equipment should not be used. All blogging activity should be done without identification to or affiliation with the Employer.

II. Social Networking

If an employee elects to maintain an account on a social networking site such as Facebook, Instagram, Twitter, or LinkedIn, it must be evident that the comments are those of the individual and are not connected with the Employer. Even if there is no connection to the Employer, you should be mindful of the tone of comments since in today's technology world, it is increasingly feasible to track the source of content to the originator. If your profile on any social networking site mentions your employment, you must be mindful of the content of the profile and its relationship to the Employer.

III. Common Sense

You are responsible for what you post. You are personally responsible for all of your online activities that can be traced in any way to the Employer. You should not be using your work email address or any Employer assets for posting or engaging in social networking or blogging activity, and should always be mindful of how your comments have the potential to impact the Employer's image and relationships with patients/clients/ prospects.

IV. Specific Guidelines When Using ______'s Name or Assets

- Be transparent (i.e., identify yourself).
- Be honest.
- Be respectful in your word usage and tone of responses/postings.
- Do not post any confidential information regarding your employment with Employer or its patients.
- If you identify the Employer, also identify your position or title.
- Include a disclaimer that any views expressed are yours and not necessarily those of the Employer or any of its patients.
- Do not post self-laudatory statements regarding your work or the work of the Employer.

- Do not post statements regarding the quality of your work or the quality of the work of the Employer.

V. **Violation of this policy can result in disciplinary action up to and including termination of employment.**

Appendix C

Online Resources

HIPAA Privacy

"Authorizations"
https://www.hhs.gov/hipaa/for-professionals/faq/authorizations/index.html

"Are there any limits or exceptions to the individual's right to have the individual's PHI sent directly to a third party?"
https://www.hhs.gov/hipaa/for-professionals/faq/2037/are-there-any-limits-or-exceptions-to-the-individuals-right/index.html

"Business Associates"
http://www.hhs.gov/hipaa/for-professionals/privacy/guidance/business-associates/

"Can an individual revoke his or her authorization?"
https://www.hhs.gov/hipaa/for-professionals/faq/474/can-an-individual-revoke-his-or-her-authorization/index.html

"Communicating with a Patient's Family, Friends, or Others Involved in the Patient's Care"
https://www.hhs.gov/sites/default/files/ocr/privacy/hipaa/understanding/coveredentities/providerffg.pdf?language=es

"Does an individual have a right under the HIPAA Privacy Rule to restrict the protected health information his or her health care provider discloses for workers' compensation purposes?"
https://www.hhs.gov/hipaa/for-professionals/faq/323/does-an-individual-have-a-right-to-restrict-protected-health-information-disclosed-for-workers-compensation/index.html

"Does the HIPAA Privacy Rule permit hospitals and other health care facilities to inform visitors or callers about a patient's location in the facility and general condition?"
https://www.hhs.gov/hipaa/for-professionals/faq/483/does-hipaa-permit-hospitals-to-inform-visitors-about-a-patients-location/index.html

"Does the HIPAA Privacy Rule preempt state laws?"
https://www.hhs.gov/hipaa/for-professionals/faq/399/does-hipaa-preempt-state-laws/index.html

"Emergency Situations: Preparedness, Planning, and Response"
https://www.hhs.gov/hipaa/for-professionals/special-topics/emergency-preparedness/index.html

"Family Members and Friends"
https://www.hhs.gov/hipaa/for-individuals/family-members-friends/index.html

"Guidance Regarding Methods for De-identification of Protected Health Information in Accordance with the Health Insurance Portability and Accountability Act (HIPAA) Privacy Rule"
https://www.hhs.gov/hipaa/for-professionals/privacy/special-topics/de-identification/index.html

"Health Information of Deceased Individuals"
https://www.hhs.gov/hipaa/for-professionals/privacy/guidance/health-information-of-deceased-individuals/index.html

"HIPAA: Handling Patient Requests for Medical Record Restriction"
https://1sthcc.com/hipaa-handling-patient-request-for-medical-record-restriction/

"HIPPA Privacy Rule Changes Address Gun Control"
https://1sthcc.com/hipaa-privacy-rule-changes-address-gun-control/

"If I am unconscious or not around, can my health care provider still share or discuss my health information with my family, friends, or others involved in my care or payment for my care?"
https://www.hhs.gov/hipaa/for-individuals/faq/524/if-i-am-unconscious-can-my-health-care-provider-still-share-my-health-information-with-family/index.html

"If I do not object, can my health care provider share or discuss my health information with my family, friends, or others involved in my care or payment for my care?"
https://www.hhs.gov/hipaa/for-individuals/faq/523/can-my-health-care-provider-share-or-discuss-my-health-information-with-my-family/index.html

Incidental Uses and Disclosures
https://www.hhs.gov/hipaa/for-professionals/privacy/guidance/incidental-uses-and-disclosures/index.html

"Individual's rights to Access PHI"
https://1sthcc.com/individuals-rights-to-access-protected-health-information/

"Individuals' Right under HIPAA to Access their Health Information"
https://www.hhs.gov/hipaa/for-professionals/privacy/guidance/access/index.html

"May a covered entity use or disclose a patient's entire medical record based on the patient's signed authorization?"
https://www.hhs.gov/hipaa/for-professionals/faq/471/may-a-covered-entity-use-or-disclose-a-patients-entire-medical-record-based-on-the-patients-authorized-signature/index.html

"May physician's offices use patient sign-in sheets or call out the names of their patients in their waiting rooms?"

https://www.hhs.gov/hipaa/for-professionals/faq/199/may-health-care-providers-use-sign-in-sheets/index.html

"Minimum Necessary"
https://www.hhs.gov/sites/default/files/ocr/privacy/hipaa/understanding/coveredentities/minimumnecessary.pdf

"Minimum Necessary Requirement"
https://www.hhs.gov/hipaa/for-professionals/privacy/guidance/minimum-necessary-requirement/index.html

"Model Notices of Privacy Practices"
https://www.hhs.gov/hipaa/for-professionals/privacy/guidance/model-notices-privacy-practices/index.html

"Notice of Privacy Practices"
https://www.hhs.gov/hipaa/for-individuals/notice-privacy-practices/index.html

"Notice of Privacy Practices for Protected Health Information"
https://www.hhs.gov/hipaa/for-professionals/privacy/guidance/privacy-practices-for-protected-health-information/index.html

"Right to an Accounting of Disclosures"
https://www.hhs.gov/hipaa/for-professionals/faq/right-to-an-accounting-of-disclosures/index.html

"Permitted Uses and Disclosures: Exchange for Healthcare Operations"
https://www.hhs.gov/sites/default/files/exchange_treatment.pdf

"Permitted Uses and Disclosures: Exchange for Treatment"
https://www.hhs.gov/sites/default/files/exchange_health_care_ops.pdf

Personal Representatives
https://www.hhs.gov/hipaa/for-professionals/privacy/guidance/personal-representatives/index.html

"Safeguards"
https://www.hhs.gov/sites/default/files/ocr/privacy/hipaa/understanding/special/healthit/safeguards.pdf

"Summary of the HIPAA Privacy Rule"
https://www.hhs.gov/hipaa/for-professionals/privacy/laws-regulations/index.html

"The HIPAA Privacy Rule"
https://www.hhs.gov/hipaa/for-professionals/privacy/index.html?language=es

"Uses and Disclosures for Treatment, Payment, and Health Care Operations"
https://www.hhs.gov/hipaa/for-professionals/privacy/guidance/disclosures-treatment-payment-health-care-operations/index.html

"What does the HIPAA Privacy Rule do?"
https://www.hhs.gov/hipaa/for-individuals/faq/187/what-does-the-hipaa-privacy-rule-do/index.html

"What does the HIPAA Privacy Rule say about a research participant's right of access to research records or results?"
https://www.hhs.gov/hipaa/for-professionals/faq/311/what-does-hipaa-say-about-research-participants-right-of-access/index.html

What is the difference between "consent" and "authorization" under the HIPAA Privacy Rule?
https://www.hhs.gov/hipaa/for-professionals/faq/264/what-is-the-difference-between-consent-and-authorization/index.html

"Why is the HIPAA Privacy Rule needed?"
https://www.hhs.gov/hipaa/for-professionals/faq/188/why-is-the-privacy-rule-needed/index.html

"Your Information. Your Rights. Our Responsibilities"
https://www.hhs.gov/sites/default/ files/ocr/privacy/ hipaa/npp_fullpage_hc_provider.pdf

HIPAA Security

"Are your mobile devices HIPAA compliant?"
https://1sthcc.com/how-secure-are-your-mobile-devices/

"Do You Meet the Security Rule Requirements for a Covered Entity?"
https://1sthcc.com/do-you-meet-the-security-rule-requirements-for-a-covered-entity/

"Does the Security Rule allow for sending electronic PHI (e-PHI) in an email or over the Internet? If so, what protections must be applied?"
https://www.hhs.gov/hipaa/for-professionals/faq/2006/does-the-security-rule-allow-for-sending-electronic-phi-in-an-email/index.html

"HIPAA Security Series #1: Security 101 for Covered Entities"
https://www.hhs.gov/sites/default/files/ocr/privacy/hipaa/administrative/securityrule/security101.pdf

"HIPAA Security Series #2: Security Standards: Administrative Safeguards"
https://www.hhs.gov/sites/default/files/ocr/privacy/hipaa/administrative/securityrule/adminsafeguards.pdf

"HIPAA Security Series #3: Security Standards: Physical Safeguards"
https://www.hhs.gov/sites/default/files/ocr/privacy/hipaa/administrative/securityrule/physsafeguards.pdf

"HIPAA Security Series #4: Security Standards: Technical Safeguards"
https://www.hhs.gov/sites/default/files/ocr/privacy/hipaa/administrative/securityrule/techsafeguards.pdf

"HIPAA Security Series #5: Security Standards: Organizational, Policies and Procedures and Documentation Requirements"
https://www.hhs.gov/sites/default/files/ocr/privacy/hipaa/administrative/securityrule/pprequirements.pdf

"HIPAA Security Series #6: Basics of Risk Analysis and Risk Management"
https://www.hhs.gov/sites/default/files/ocr/privacy/hipaa/administrative/securityrule/riskassessment.pdf

"How can a small provider implement the standards in Security Rule?"
https://www.hhs.gov/hipaa/for-professionals/faq/2007/how-can-a-small-provider-implement-the-standards-in-security-rule/index.html

"Is the use of encryption mandatory in the Security Rule?"
https://www.hhs.gov/hipaa/for-professionals/faq/2001/is-the-use-of-encryption-mandatory-in-the-security-rule/index.html

"Security Risk Assessment (SRA) Tool User Guide"
https://www.healthit.gov/sites/default/files/attachmenta-security_risk_assessment_tool_user_guide_v6.pdf

"Summary of the HIPAA Security Rule"
https://www.hhs.gov/hipaa/for-professionals/security/laws-regulations/index.html

"The Security Rule"
https://www.hhs.gov/hipaa/for-professionals/security/index.html?language=es

"What does the Security Rule require a covered entity to do to comply with the Security Incidents Procedures standard?"
https://www.hhs.gov/hipaa/for-professionals/faq/2002/what-does-the-security-rule-require-a-covered-entity-to-do-to-comply/index.html

"What is the difference between addressable and required implementation specifications in the Security Rule?"
https://www.hhs.gov/hipaa/for-professionals/faq/2020/what-is-the-difference-between-addressable-and-required-implementation-specifications/index.html

"Why is the HIPAA Security Rule needed and what is the purpose of the security standards?"
https://www.hhs.gov/hipaa/for-professionals/faq/2000/why-is-hipaa-needed-and-what-is-the-purpose-of-security-standards/index.html

HIPAA Breach Notification

"Breach Notification Rule"
https://www.hhs.gov/hipaa/for-professionals/breach-notification/index.html

"Chapter 7: Breach Notification, HIPAA Enforcement, and Other Laws and Requirements"
https://www.healthit.gov/sites/default/files/playbook/pdf/breach-notification-hipaa-enforcement-and-other-laws-and-requirements.pdf

"Notice to the Secretary of HHS: Breach of Unsecured Protected Health Information"
https://ocrportal.hhs.gov/ocr/breach/wizard_breach.jsf? faces-redirect=true

"Submitting Notice of a Breach to the Secretary"
https://www.hhs.gov/hipaa/for-professionals/breach-notification/breach-reporting/index.html

HIPAA Enforcement

"All Case Examples"
https://www.hhs.gov/hipaa/for-professionals/compliance-enforcement/examples/all-cases/index.html#case26

"Enforcement Data"
https://www.hhs.gov/hipaa/for-professionals/compliance-enforcement/data/index.html

"Enforcement Highlights"
https://www.hhs.gov/hipaa/for-professionals/compliance-enforcement/data/enforcement-highlights/index.html

"HIPAA Enforcement"
https://www.hhs.gov/hipaa/for-professionals/compliance-enforcement/

"HIPAA Privacy, Security, and Breach Notification Audit Program"
https://www.hhs.gov/hipaa/for-professionals/compliance-enforcement/audit/index.html

"OCR Launches Phase 2 of HIPAA Audit Program"
https://www.hhs.gov/hipaa/for-professionals/compliance-enforcement/audit/phase2announcement/index.html

"The HIPAA Enforcement Rule"
https://www.hhs.gov/hipaa/for-professionals/special-topics/enforcement-rule/index.html

Related HIPAA Resources

"Business Associate Contracts"
https://www.hhs.gov/hipaa/for-professionals/covered-entities/sample-business-associate-agreement-provisions/index.html

"Consequences for HIPAA violations don't stop when a business closes"
https://www.hhs.gov/hipaa/for-professionals/compliance-enforcement/agreements/filefax/index.html

"Guide to Privacy and Security of Health Information"
https://www.healthit.gov/sites/default/files/pdf/privacy/onc_privacy_and_security_chapter4_v1_022112.pdf

"HIPAA: Handling Patient Requests for Medical Record Restriction"
https://1sthcc.com/hipaa-handling-patient-request-for-medical-record-restriction/

"HIPAA Facts for Professionals"
https://www.hhs.gov/ hipaa/for-professionals/faq

"HIPAA Privacy & HIPAA Security; Question: What is the difference between HIPAA Privacy and HIPAA Security?"
https://privacy.wv.gov/tips/Pages/HIPAAPrivacyHIPAASecurity.aspx

"HITECH Act Enforcement Interim Final Rule"
https://www.hhs.gov/hipaa/for-professionals/special-topics/hitech-act-enforcement-interim-final-rule/index.html

"How to File a Health Information Privacy or Security Complaint"
https://www.hhs.gov/hipaa/filing-a-complaint/complaint-process/index.html?language=es

"How to Prevent HIPAA Violations"
https://1sthcc.com/how-to-prevent-hipaa-violations/

"Is a covered entity liable for, or required to monitor, the actions of its business associates?"
https://www.hhs.gov/hipaa/for-professionals/faq/236/covered-entity-liable-for-action/index.html

"Is Your Business Associate Prepared for a Security Incident?"
https://www.hhs.gov/sites/default/files/hipaa-cyber-awareness-monthly-issue-4.pdf?language=es

"Joint Guidance on the Application of the Family Educational Rights and Privacy Act (FERPA) And the Health Insurance Portability and Accountability Act of 1996 (HIPAA) To Student Health Records"
https://www2.ed.gov/policy/gen/guid/fpco/doc/ferpa-hipaa-guidance.pdf

"Message to Our Nation's Health Care Providers"
https://www.hhs.gov/sites/default/files/ocr/office/lettertonationhcp.pdf

"Mobile Device Privacy and Security"
https://archive.healthit.gov/providers-professionals/five-steps-organizations-can-take-manage-mobile-devices-used-health-care-pro

"My entity just experienced a cyber-attack! What do we do now?"
https://www.hhs.gov/sites/default/files/cyber-attack-checklist-06-2017.pdf

"Omnibus HIPAA Rulemaking"
https://www.hhs.gov/hipaa/for-professionals/privacy/laws-regulations/combined-regulation-text/omnibus-hipaa-rulemaking/index.html

U.S. Department of Health & Human Services
https://www.hhs.gov/

"SAMHSA finalizes changes to clarify health privacy rules for people who seek substance use disorder treatment"
https://www.samhsa.gov/newsroom/press-announcements/201801021100

"Your Rights Under HIPAA"
https://www.hhs.gov/hipaa/for-individuals/guidance-materials-for-consumers/index.html

www.ingramcontent.com/pod-product-compliance
Lightning Source LLC
LaVergne TN
LVHW070952210926
848482LV00002B/186